MUSIC
AND RELIGION

AMS PRESS
NEW YORK

MUSIC
AND RELIGION

Edited by
STANLEY ARMSTRONG HUNTER

Introduction
CLARENCE DICKINSON

THE ABINGDON PRESS
NEW YORK   CINCINNATI   CHICAGO

Library of Congress Cataloging in Publication Data

Hunter, Stanley Armstrong, 1888-   ed.
   Music and religion.

   Fifteen sermons, by ministers of various communions,
on the value of music in the conduct of worship.
Cf. Pref.
   1. Church music. 2. Music--Analysis, appreciation.
3. Music in churches. I. Title.
ML3001.H86 1973   783'.08   72-1615
ISBN 0-404-08316-1

Reprinted from a copy in the collections
of the Newark Public Library

From the edition of 1930, New York and Cincinnati
First AMS edition published in 1973
Manufactured in United States of America

AMS PRESS INC.
NEW YORK, N.Y. 10003

Dedicated to E. P. H.

"All we have willed or hoped or dreamed of good
    shall exist;
    Not its semblance, but itself; no beauty, nor
      good, nor power
Whose voice has gone forth, but each survives
    for the melodist
    When Eternity affirms the conception of an
      hour.
The high that proved too high, the heroic for
    earth too hard,
    The passion that left the ground to lose itself
      in the sky,
Are music sent up to God by the lover and the
    bard;
    Enough that he heard it once: we shall hear it
      by and by."

   —From Abt Vogler, by Robert Browning.

CONTENTS

A PRAYER

By Lloyd Cassel Douglas

Our Father God, to whom all praise and honor should be given among men, we thank thee for the high gift of music whereby our hearts are uplifted to realms beyond this world of toil and care.

For the genius of all who have interpreted heavenly mysteries to us through this ethereal agency, we thank thee.

For the response we find within ourselves to the appeal of music we give thee praise.

Attune our hearts to the symphony of thy heavenly grace, that we may evermore understand thy will for us in our daily lives, and realize increasingly the peace thou wouldst have us bear in our souls.

Teach us to praise thee with all our hearts and lives; thou who art forever holy.

Through Jesus Christ, our Lord. Amen.

PREFACE

ONE of the outstanding trends in the religious life of our day is a new emphasis upon the conduct of public worship. Increasing attention is being paid to this peculiar function of the Christian Church. That which differentiates the church from other institutions of our modern life is worship, which Professor Henry Nelson Wieman claims to be "the only suitable preparation for the greatest creative artistry in all the world, the art of reshaping the total vital process of living."

This book grew out of a desire on the part of one pastor to discover from ministers in his own and other fellowships of faith what value they placed upon music in the conduct of worship and what ideas they might share regarding its bearing on religion. The suggestion was first made to a few friends that each preach a sermon on this theme at a musical service.

Fifteen ministers responded with contributions, most of which were specially prepared for this collection, and then preached to their own congregations; some of the sermons, however, had been delivered previously on special occasions. The layman who contributed the introduction presides at the organ at the daily chapel services of Union Theological Seminary, and teaches in its School of Sacred Music. He is a composer of note whose influence on church music has been marked.

The preparation of this book has revealed how widespread is the desire on the part of ministers to make the best use of God's gift of music for the purposes of true religion. As Dr. William P. Merrill has well said: "In the long and varied story of man's soul development, music holds an honored place. It is the one art which has maintained a close intimacy with religion, and has always filled an indispensable place in worship. There is nothing in the vast realm of man's interests so closely akin to his religion as his music. Music can render to the soul of man to-day, in its efforts to find expression for its most real and deep feelings, an immeasurable service, needed as never before. For it is characteristic of the religious life of the present that it distrusts definitions and formulas, yet craves expression. Music comes nearer than anything else man knows to expressing the inexpressible."

That the Bible has much to say about music is evident from the widely scattered Scripture verses selected as texts. Curiously enough, only two writers happened to choose the same text.

Each contributor was asked to designate his favorite hymn. It is interesting to note that "O Love That Wilt Not Let Me Go" was chosen by two pastors in different communions. Two others selected "Dear Lord and Father of Mankind," a hymn by Whittier, a member of the Society of Friends, who do not use music or hymns in worship. No denominational lines are drawn in our hymnals, and in the praise of the sanctuary we already have an expression of real unity.

Hymns written by five of the contributors to the symposium are included.

It is hoped that this book will make worshipers and ministers more deeply appreciative of the heritage of our best hymns, and more eager to improve congregational singing, which is sadly neglected in our land. "How anyone can hope for artistic worship in which there is the singing of jig-tune hymns is past understanding," exclaims Bernard Iddings Bell in his chapter on "The Art of Worship," in *Beyond Agnosticism*. He adds, "One of the first steps in the restoration of worship will be large bonfires of trashy hymnals."

One agrees with his conclusion that worship is an art "that all humanitarian persons should be willing to sacrifice much to promote, for it has within it the possibility of making the dull gray of human living shine through and through with the prismatic beauties of God."

All royalties from this book, a co-operative undertaking, will be given to the library of Ewing Christian College, Allahabad, India.

STANLEY ARMSTRONG HUNTER.

St. John's Presbyterian Church,
   Berkeley, California.

INTRODUCTION

THERE has never been a time when the music in the church service or music in relation to religion has received so much attention as at present. To this the very publication of such a book as MUSIC AND RELIGION bears testimony. A publisher told me a short time ago that his house had brought out what they considered a rather remarkable book of studies of various themes for services, including short lists of musical numbers appropriate for use with these themes, and that he had been greatly surprised to find that these lists of music constituted the book's strongest selling point.

Only a few years ago anyone who could play the piano a bit was considered eligible for the post of organist in most churches, and any so-called sacred music might be sung, provided only that it was not altogether too involved to be attempted by the quartet or at the irregular rehearsals of the "faithful few" who made up the choir. Now all this is changed, or changing. On almost all church bulletins there appears the name of the minister of music—or organist and choirmaster—

and ceremonies of installation are becoming
more usual in connection with his appoint-
ment.   From among the church attendants or
membership, where such a thing is feasible,
singing groups of different ages are organized
to lead in the worship through song, sepa-
rately or together.   Many a church has, indeed, found this a most effective means of
building up its membership and of increasing
attendance upon its services.   The young people—and the older people as well—can be interested in the singing to the extent that they
will make laws for themselves which will in-
sure their presence at the services, and this
will attract also their friends from within and
without the church.   And they will be attracted not merely for entertainment such as
the church may furnish occasionally, nor for
something in which they are only onlookers—
now present, now absent—but for a definite
service which they will render with pride and
joy.   The recognition of this has been so keen
within the last few years that I know of
churches in which from a tenth to a fifth of
the membership is organized into choirs. The
Children's Choir movement has spread beyond
the bounds of Choir School and Friendly Society, until we find towns in which all the children are organized into choirs, irrespective of

any denominational affiliation, and are proving a powerful aid in the movement toward church unity or the community church.

But this spirit need not be peculiar to voluntary choral organizations; it can and should distinguish every choir. The organist and choirmaster who is truly a minister of music should endeavor to make the choir realize the service it renders to the church and the service it can render through music to God and to his children.

To encourage and in some measure to give direction and guidance to this mounting interest in church music, the churches are, one after another, appointing commissions to study the music offered in our churches, to examine hymnals and anthems and to consider how to utilize to the best advantage the musical resources of every kind of church. The results of these studies are set forth from time to time in services given for conferences of ministers, musicians, and the laity. Schools are being established for the training of ministers of music. Union Theological Seminary, for example, has been so impressed with the need of such a trained ministry that it has established its School of Sacred Music in which courses are given in everything pertaining to the ministry of music in the church.

In it the students also take the studies prescribed for those who are preparing for the preaching ministry—courses pertaining to the Life of Christ, the Literature of the Bible, Church History, and kindred subjects, which will broaden and deepen their understanding of and feeling for the church and its Master whom they serve.

And all this to what end? That through the use of music at once beautiful and appropriate, each service of worship may be skillfully unified into a perfect whole, as the expression of one idea or the illumination of one element or thought in worship, so that the effect of the service may be emotionally intensified and exalted through beauty and through music's direct appeal to the hearts of men. We are coming once again to the realization of the power of this direct appeal and the exaltation that rests in beauty. In the early days of church worship, influenced by the Pilgrim Fathers and the Puritans, beauty was excluded, as it was viewed with distrust, and morality received the whole weight of emphasis. For some time back these accents have been growing fainter and a new emphasis has been placed on doing, rather than on being, on thought for one's fellow men, and not for one's own righteousness. The emphasis has been transferred to social service, which has even come near superseding worship.

And now we have come once again to the perception that, to be effective and faithful, morality and social service alike must spring steadily from an inner source; and we realize that this source must be kept deep, rich, and living. As powerful agents in effecting this we have come to recognize beauty and emotion. Men are moved by their emotions more swiftly and intensely than through any other channel. Down deep within the heart of them they are charged with something hidden, unplumbed, which, when stirred, and then brought under the direction of moral energy, may express itself in great deeds or faithful service for the furtherance of the glory of God and good will toward men.

To these deep emotional springs music makes its appeal. Reformers and evangelists and leaders of religious movements from early Christian times, through Huss and Luther to the Salvation Army, have always been keenly alive to the use of music as a great power to open the hearts of men to their message and to emphasize and illumine that message. Now the organized church is slowly becoming more definitely conscious of this, and is devoting more attention to the subject of sacred music than at any time in its history. To the furtherance of increasing study and interest this book is an exceedingly important contribution.

CLARENCE DICKINSON.

Union Theological Seminary,
New York City.

HENRY VAN DYKE, dean of American letters, is the author of several hymns which are enriching year after year the worship of an increasing number of churches. In the Presbyterian Church, of which he is a minister, he was chairman of the General Assembly's committee which prepared the *Book of Common Worship,* officially adopted in 1902. The book has been of great value in enhancing the dignity and inspiration of worship in many Presbyterian churches.

Several of Doctor van Dyke's inimitable stories deal with themes connected with music. He has not neglected the treatment of music in his poetry. In his *Collected Verse* many a music lover will give first place to his poem on "Music." A quotation from it closes the contribution which follows.

Doctor van Dyke accepted the call of the Brick Church, New York City, in 1883, after a three-year pastorate of the United Congregational Church of Newport, Rhode Island. He remained until 1900, when he became professor of English literature at Princeton University. He was frequently called upon to occupy his former pulpit. Music of the highest type contributed to the helpfulness of the Brick Church services.

He was elected moderator of the General Assembly in 1902, and at the present time is chairman of the committee on the Revision of the *Book of Common Worship.*

A son of the Rev. Henry J. van Dyke, he was graduated from Princeton in 1873, and remained for three years in Princeton Theological Seminary. Many universities have conferred upon him honorary degrees, of which Oxford's D. C. L. in 1917 is one of the most cherished.

His son, the Rev. Tertius van Dyke, now of the Congregational Church, Washington, Connecticut, has collaborated with him in some later writings.

Over a score of volumes justify his sustained reputation.

Favorite Hymn. "You ask me to name my favorite hymn," he writes. "It is difficult, because there are two points of view from which hymns may be considered. As poetry I should probably choose 'Lead, Kindly Light,' with 'Jerusalem the Golden' as next best. As a hymn to be sung by a congregation, 'How Firm a Foundation' stands first with me, and 'O Jesus, I Have Promised' stands next to it."

JOYFUL, JOYFUL, WE ADORE THEE

HENRY VAN DYKE

Tune, *The Hymn to Joy*

Joyful, joyful, we adore thee,
  God of glory, Lord of love;
Hearts unfold like flowers before thee,
  Opening to the sun above.
Melt the clouds of sin and sadness,
  Drive the dark of doubt away,
Giver of immortal gladness,
  Fill us with the light of day.

All thy works with joy surround thee,
  Earth and heaven reflect thy rays,
Stars and angels sing around thee,
  Center of unbroken praise.
Field and forest, vale and mountain,
  Flowery meadow, flashing sea,
Chanting bird and flowing fountain,
  Call us to rejoice in thee.

Thou art giving and forgiving,
  Ever blessing, ever blest,
Well-spring of the joy of living,
  Ocean-depth of happy rest!
Thou our Father, Christ our Brother,
  All who live in love are thine;
Teach us how to love each other,
  Lift us to the Joy Divine.

Mortals, join the mighty chorus
   Which the morning stars began;
Father love is reigning o'er us,
   Brother love binds man to man.
Ever singing, march we onward,
   Victors in the midst of strife,
Joyful music leads us Sunward
   In the triumph song of life.

I

MUSIC AS AN AID TO FAITH

PREACHED AT THE DEDICATION OF THE NEW CHAPEL
AT MERCERSBURG ACADEMY

MUSIC is the art which modulates and combines sounds to express emotion.

Like poetry, it has its birth in a quickened feeling.

We human beings are subject to strange stirrings of the heart, mysterious and invisible, which find involuntary bodily expression in pulses hastened or delayed, muscles tensed or relaxed, eyes brightened or dimmed, faces paled or flushed with color. When our feelings rise into the realm of consciousness they naturally seek an utterance in poetry or in music. Often these twin-born arts join hand in hand and move together in their revelation of what is most intimate, secret, and vital in the life of the spirit.

There is a difference in the means by which these two arts fulfill their purpose. The medium through which poetry works is language. Words which are full of meaning, symbols of ideas, made significant by human use, made beautiful or potent by the magic of memory and association—words are the material in which the poet clothes the children of his imagination. But if the quickened emotion is not present, either in fact or in memory, the words are dead. The so-called poem will be no more poetical than a section of the catechism, an auctioneer's catalogue, or the advertisement of a new tooth paste.

The medium through which music works is pure sound. Tones not articulate nor definitely attached to certain ideas, but ordered and arranged in certain relations of pitch and volume and rhythm out of which melody and harmony are born—these are the elements from which the musician evolves his creation for the hearing ear.

Again, as in poetry, it is the quickened emotion which is vital, indispensable, life-giving. Unfelt music is barren. Only when the heart is moved is music born alive.

The relations of sounds which make them capable of being woven together into music are mysterious; but they are certainly governed by laws as sure, as reasonable, as wonderful, as the laws which govern the colors in light. The learned student of physics and mathematics knows these laws, at least in part, and can express them in figures and diagrams.

But the soul of music, moving within its laws, is something more than they. It is revealed by instinct to the shepherd lad as he plays on his pipe

> ". . . the tune all the sheep know, as one
>   after one,
> So docile, they come to the pen-door till folding
>   is done."

It is discerned in contemplation by the great composer as

> ". . . the symphony builds up its round
> Full sweep of architectural harmony
> Above the tide of time."

But always it is the same, this soul of music— an impulse obedient to a control, an ordered freedom, a self expressed in harmony with others.

Now, this is why I have ventured to speak of music as an aid to faith. The very existence of music is an argument for God. In a world of chance, a chaos of unreason and deaf power, music could never be, nor could we feel its influence.

Wisely did the poet Collins, in his "Ode on the Passions," write of "Music, *heavenly* maid." Wisely did Carlyle say, "Music is the

speech of angels." Wisely does the book of
Job describe creation as the time when *"the
morning stars sang together, and all the sons
of God shouted for joy."* Wisely and by inspiration does the Apocalypse tell us that the
Heavenly City is full of song—*"a new song,"*
Saint John calls it—high and holy and immortal.

Here on earth, in human use, the ministry
of music is manifold. All our feelings and
emotions—yes, even our physical sensations—
may be expressed in music and are subject to
its influence. It follows therefore that like
all the other arts it may be degraded, per-
verted to base uses, and made the handmaid
of folly, sensuality, and beastliness. Evil music may go as far down in the way of vice as
good music may rise high in the path of virtue.

There are musical drugs and intoxicants
that loosen all the sinews of self-control, and
stir the sensual passions to a wild and fatal
excess. They beat and hammer upon the
nerves with savage discords. They strum and
tinkle fantastic allurements to transient and
debasing pleasures. They agitate their victims with convulsive movement and leave
them, when the Circean enchantment dies,
shamed and exhausted.

The upward and the downward path in mu-

sic may be traced most clearly in a primitive
and undeveloped race like the Negroes. Their
jazz-tunes represent the tendency to revert to
barbarism, in which many foolish white folks
seem inclined to follow them. Their Negro-
spirituals breathe, in strangely moving tones
and cadences, the aspiration and yearning of
a retarded and oppressed race toward beauty,
peace, and freedom of soul.

The poet Lanier said of true music, "It is
love in search of a word." I think it is also
worship putting on her garment of praise.

It is not strange that the highest musical
development has been associated with religion.
Faith, if it be real, calls forth the deepest and
most enduring emotion of the human spirit.
Music is an aid to faith because it utters that
emotion in forms of beauty which linger in
the memory long after they have faded on the
ear.

A church without music is like a bird without wings. Let the organ send its uplifting
waves of sound through the arches. Let the
full-voiced choir enrich the air with stately
anthem and sweet voluntary. Let the whole
congregation worship heartily in psalms and
hymns and spiritual songs. Let the joy of
Christian faith utter itself in noble music;
for an increase of joy in religion is the thing

that the church most needs to-day to draw
men to her.

Music, in thee we float.
And lose the lonely note
Of self in thy divinely ordered strain,
Until at last we find
The life to love resigned
In harmony of joy restored again;
And songs that cheered our mortal days
Break on the shore of light in endless hymns of
praise.

RUSSELL HENRY STAFFORD in 1927 was chosen to succeed Dr. George A. Gordon in the historic pulpit of Old South Church, Boston, Massachusetts, after a happy pastorate of four years in the Pilgrim Church of Saint Louis.

A native of Wisconsin, a student at the University of California, a graduate of the University of Minnesota and Drew University, with an assistant pastorate in Central Congregational Church, Brooklyn, New York, and two pastorates in Minneapolis, he brought with him to Boston wide knowledge of religious conditions in other centers.

In 1923 he wrote *Finding God,* and has recently published *Christian Humanism,* a book which reveals an incisive mind and genial spirit.

He is a trustee of Drury College, Iberia Academy, Piedmont College of Demorest, Georgia, and Anatolia College at Salonica, Greece.

Chicago Theological Seminary conferred the D. D. degree upon him in 1924.

Favorite Hymn: "Lord, Speak to Me That I May Speak," by Miss Frances Ridley Havergal. "This hymn was sung at my ordination to the tune 'Holley,' in Central Church, Brooklyn, New York, in May, 1924, and is regularly sung in my church by the congregation at the service nearest the anniversary of that ordination."

II

THE MEANING OF MUSIC

I ASSUME that we are all lovers of music. But have you ever undertaken to formulate the reasons why music means so much to us? In the thought that such an attempt may lead us into fuller appreciation of the privilege we have in modern America of enjoying music at its best, I invite you to consider with me, as a fellow amateur, the rudiments of a philosophy of music.

In the first place, how does there come to be music? It is born of mankind's appreciative response to our environment. We live in a singing world. Nature is full of music. The soughing of winds, the ripple of streams, the roar of waterfalls, the calls of birds—these are about us in the wild places. And in the places of men's habitation the very noises which, near at hand, disturb us sometimes, blend at a distance into weird and subtle harmonies. If, for instance, on any height overlooking any city, you will hearken to the murmur of the town, you will find that all the jarring notes of traffic and manufacture are mutually attuned in a sustained and soothing flow of sound, just as great choral effects can be produced from large choirs in which many voices are defective. Moreover, to sing is as instinctive with mankind as to breathe, in the natural order, or to believe, in the psychic order. Children often sing before they talk. It would be as impossible to find a people without music as to find a people without faith. These things spring from the depths of human consciousness, and are inseparable from its development.

And what functions does music perform in our personal and group life? First, music is a channel of self-expression. That is to say, we have moods and feelings which can be expressed only through fitting kinds of sound, and which it would be detrimental to our well-being to repress, if not fatal to our sanity. When men mourn, they chant their grief; so we have the dirge—a regularized moan, so to speak—and such meters as the *qinah* in Hebrew and the elegiac in English verse, marking the intention that poetry with such syllabic arrangements be set to melancholy melody. When men rejoice, also, they sing— whence the jubilant pæans in all tongues. When men fight, they sing; soldiers endure discomforts and brave perils with light heart to the accompaniment of stirring battle-cries and marching-songs. When men pray, they sing: the hymns of all centuries have been prayers in song form, bearing men's souls upon the wings of their melodies to the very throne of God. There is indeed blessedness in the possession and use of this means of outlet for emotions for which no words could be adequate.

Second, music inspires feelings and moods which men need to experience in certain circumstances or relations. Sometimes music is misused to call up states of mind and heart which were best buried in oblivion, as when the war spirit is inflamed by the windy argument of brass bands. But, employed with worthy purpose, music is a voice calling us to life's noblest and most generous aims and endeavors. Consider how the mood of worship is brought to ascendancy over great congregations by such hymns as

> "O for a thousand tongues to sing
> My great Redeemer's praise!"

Consider how the heroism of a justly embattled nation is evoked by patriotic songs. Consider how your mental tone has often been changed from depression to gladness by some light and cheering air. Music is thus an instrument for calling forth appropriate tones of the soul and sometimes of release from baneful moods.

Third, music, as we often remark, "takes us into another world." Listening to deep, strange harmonies, we become aware of reaches of potential presence and contact, of realms of thought and emotion, lying far beneath and above the humdrum plane of our normal consciousness; and by this new awareness we are led to understand that life is doubtless infinitely greater than it appears to our workaday senses. I cannot describe this adventure of the discovery of new worlds through music to him who has not had it, but I am confident that there are but few who have not had the experience.

Of course some other experiences have a like effect upon us. I remember, for instance, an ether-dream from which I have carried, through the years ever since, a conviction amounting to certainty that life as we live it here is simply one plane, and by no means an especially significant one, in an infinite gradation of the levels of reality, as we are some day to know it through and through. And it happens that for me, probably because of certain early associations, the reading of classical Greek opens a secret door into an ever bright world of sunlight and youth. But, whereas we may severally find private portals like these into enriched comprehension of the magnitudes of life, for all men everywhere music is such a portal. In other words, it is a revelation of God, a prophecy of the eternally real, giving us a direct acquaintance with regions of subtle charm and of inexhaustible hope which our reason can only faintly and vaguely conceive, and can never explore or explain.

Thus music, welling up from the depths of the human soul as a native impulse inseparable from our very consciousness, and instructed in its forms by the melodies of nature about us, serves us in at least three ways: to give outlet to moods which it were dangerous to stifle; to incite moods which it is good to entertain; to unveil heights and depths in life not otherwise accessible to our observation. We have, then, reason to be grateful for the increased opportunities of musical enjoyment which have come to us of late. I remember that some years ago it seemed very wonderful to me to sit by a grate fire in a log cabin, at the very verge of an unbroken Northern forest near the Canadian border, and listen to a phonograph discoursing opera and symphony. But it is much more wonderful now to be able to listen, in such frontier cabins, to great musicians, at the very moment when they are actually performing, in far-distant cities. Moreover, church music has been steadily improving in this country of late years; and the support of other good music presented by choral societies and symphony orchestras has almost incalculably increased, so that he who will may feast upon fine music in any city of the land.

Our thanks for this are due, of course, to the musicians themselves and to generous patrons of this art who underwrite the costs of major developments in its presentation to the public. But most of all we owe gratitude to God, for having implanted in our bosoms that impulse of song which in these manifold expressions becomes so potent an agency of magnified vision and deepened understanding of the meaning of life. And we ought, in the rush of this hurrying world and among the myriad distractions of business from the high concerns of the soul, to cultivate our innate capacities of musical expression and appreciation as veritable gifts of God. Of course it is possible to be musical without being holy; but I question whether it be possible to be holy— to enjoy that intimate, unwavering, inescapable conviction of the reality of things unseen, which is the foundation of noble character—without appreciation of music, which is one of the most precious of instrumentalities of the life of conscious communion with heaven and willing devotion to heaven's service.

So I urge that we accredit high value to the wondrous impressions which music makes upon our souls, and that we open our lives more widely to its ministries; that by it we may be led into a deeper apprehension of life's spiritual dimensions than can be attained in any other way universally accessible, and may thereby be strengthened for our burdens and made courageous in our troubles, as servants of God in this singing world—this terrestrial overture to the symphonic adoration of the Most High in his everlasting dwelling place.

WILLIAM PIERSON MERRILL, minister since 1911 of the Brick Church on Fifth Avenue, New York, is not only the author of several hymns that have found their way into modern hymnals, but is also the composer of some hymn tunes of wide acceptance. An accomplished musician himself, he has maintained the high standards of music for which the Brick Church has long been famous. With Clarence Dickinson, his organist and choir director, there has existed ideal co-operation.

A graduate of Rutgers College and Union Theological Seminary, he went to Chestnut Hill, Philadelphia, as pastor of the Trinity Church for five years. From 1895 to 1911 he served the Sixth Presbyterian Church of Chicago, in which city his ministry has taken deep root. He holds honorary degrees from Rutgers, New York, and Columbia Universities.

Doctor Merrill has been president of the World Alliance for International Friendship, and as might be expected echoes of his abiding interest in world peace and good will resound in this sermon.

He has been president since 1915 of the trustees of the Church Peace Union, founded by his friend Andrew Carnegie. His books have been many. Among the titles are: *Faith Building, Faith and Sight, Footings for Faith, Christian Internationalism, The Common Creed of Christians, The Freedom of the Preacher, Liberal Christianity,* and *Prophets of the Dawn.*

Favorite Hymn: "On the whole I think I make more use of Whittier's 'Dear Lord and Father of Mankind' than of any hymn in my personal religious life. I greatly admire also 'When I Survey the Wondrous Cross.'"

RISE UP, O MEN OF GOD!

WILLIAM PIERSON MERRILL

Tune, *St. Thomas*

Rise up, O men of God!
  Have done with lesser things;
Give heart and soul and mind and strength
  To serve the King of kings.

Rise up, O men of God!
  His kingdom tarries long;
Bring in the day of brotherhood
  And end the night of wrong.

Rise up, O men of God!
  The church for you doth wait,
Her strength unequal to her task;
  Rise up, and make her great!

Lift high the cross of Christ!
  Tread where his feet have trod;
As brothers of the Son of man
  Rise up, O men of God!
        (Reprinted by permission of author.)

III

THE PARABLE OF HARMONY

Text: Thy will be done in earth as it is in heaven.—*Matt. 6. 10.*

RELIGION has much to learn from music, for religion deals with life, and music is the most perfect symbol of life. Among all the interests of mankind no two are nearer together than music and religion. Those who appreciate music are quick to perceive that the principles on which it is based are the very principles of life itself. Even in the days of its crude beginnings music was felt by great thinkers—Plato, Confucius, and others—to be of supreme moral and religious value. Plato might exclude poets from his Republic, but not musicians. The Hebrew feared the influence of other forms of art, but he made large and free use of music.

Emerson tells us that

"In the mud and scum of things,
    There alway, alway something sings."

Thomas Carlyle, grim apostle of reality, in whose life and work is little enough of rhythm

41

and smoothness, speaks of the music ever to be found at the heart of things. Michael Pupin, leading scientist, puts the meaning of the whole process of evolution in the phrase, "From chaos to cosmos." The world is moving on toward harmony, out of chaos into order, God's majestic purpose marking the melody and rhythm through the ages, the acts and thoughts of men and nations working out the counterpoint, until this tiny planet plays its part with perfect accord in the music of the spheres.

"From chaos to cosmos." That is our path. And music illustrates and illumines the way as nothing else can do. The problem of each individual life is how to bring order, the divine order and harmony, into the seething chaos of conflicting interests, passions, impulses, and thoughts which make up the inner life. The problem of social life is the same problem of order and harmony; how to bring groups, classes, nations, the world, "from chaos to cosmos," out of the danger and misery of disorder into the beauty of perfect harmony. How can it be done?

There is a beautiful parable to be found in the way harmony and the beauty of perfect order are attained in the realm of music. Every true song and symphony is an illustration, for the glory of great music lies in the perfect blending, in an artistic whole, of many voices and themes. It is essentially a venture in co-operation. Best of all do we see the true meaning and promise of perfect and lasting order in our common social life when we watch a mighty chorus or great orchestra at work, and see how it achieves that perfect harmony which delights the soul. How can human life become truly harmonious, blending in one mighty choral symphony of righteousness and peace and joy in the Holy Spirit?

Let us imagine ourselves in some hall where an orchestra is about to play. What confusion reigns at the beginning! Members of the orchestra stroll in upon the stage, walk about, seat themselves, one here, one there; gradually the seats upon the stage are filled. But each man seems busy with his own thoughts and themes. There is a tuning of instruments, a running over of motives and bits of difficult work, discordant in the extreme, interesting only because it suggests the harmony that is to come.

How that resembles our ordinary life and ways! So much of our social ongoing is marked by discord, by unrelated acts and purposes, men and groups jostling one another, each separate ideal and effort thrusting its way through a mass of opposing or unrelated ideals and efforts. Some believe in and uphold a principle of "unrestricted competition." They are like the savage chief who visited one of the European countries, and, after listening to a symphony concert, said he liked best "the very first time they played." He meant the discordant, individualistic process of tuning up!

But wise men and women are beginning to see that it is imperative that our whole social order move out from the "tuning up" stage of unrestricted individualism to true co-operation. How shall it be done? Look again at what happens in the music hall.

All in a moment a change comes. The conductor enters and raises his baton. There is silence, and then all together swing into some majestic movement, the volume of perfect harmony rising aloft and bearing our thoughts and emotions with it into a higher world of joy.

There is a picture of human life. The distracted, discordant scene at the opening is a picture of our life as it is. The unity and harmony is a picture of our life as it should be. Our social life, of man with man, of nation with nation, should form a mighty harmony, a symphony of glad praise and mighty purpose, of loving acts and righteous conduct, all forming a harmonious whole, a choral symphony, rising to the glory of God and for the delight of God's world.

It is far from that at present. From society as now constituted rises a babel of discordant voices and sounds. We are still in the tuning-up stage. How can the harmony come? Let music answer. First, it comes through each individual filling his own place and playing his own part rightly. That is the foundation of perfect harmony. If one instrument is missing, if one player stumbles or falls in his part, the perfect harmony is spoiled. Each has his place assigned him by the leader, each has his part marked in the score, each must stay at his post and do his duty.

The foundation of that perfect harmony we hope to realize in human society is also that each stay in his own place and play his part rightly. Do not think your part so little that you can drop out and not be missed. Every note is essential to perfect harmony. Each is needed by the whole. Browning has a beautiful poem about a boy who every day at his work sang a little song of praise. The boy was raised to the high office of Pope and in his engrossing business the little song was forgotten; but God felt the loss of that note in the harmony of creation, insignificant though it was. There is truth in the poem. If your life, if mine, however humble, fails to fill its place and play its part, God misses something from the divine harmony he loves to hear rising from his world. If you want the perfect harmony to come, stay at your post, learn your part well, and play it rightly with joy and grace.

But though this is the foundation of the harmony, it is far from being all that is necessary to it. Every player might play his individual part well and yet the result be discord, if each played as and when he pleased. The second condition of harmony is that each subordinate his own playing to the meaning and beauty of the whole. All must be playing the same composition if you would have harmony; yes, and the same arrangement of it. How dreadful the discord, if every member of chorus or orchestra should bring the composition he or she wanted to sing or to play and all should try to sing or play them together! Did you ever hear a Chinese band? That is just the effect it produces on us. They agree on a theme, and then each plays away as he wants to, coming in when he pleases, wandering off to other themes if he chooses. We could not stand such music. Yet, my friends, that is the sort of music we too often make in our lives. God hears just such discords, for we are selfish. We will play our own themes, in our own way, whether they fit into the world-theme or not. And so, though we live our lives well enough, they make discord, not harmony, as each lives his own life in his own way.

Here lies the danger of the era in which we are now living, with its exaggerated emphasis on the importance and value of unlimited individual self-expression. It may be that in the past there has been too much constraint, too great a tendency to cramp our freedom by strait-jackets of conventionality. But the true type of that order of civilization we hope to attain is not a Chinese Band, but a Symphony Orchestra. Unless individual instincts, impulses, and desires are fully and cheerfully subordinated to the general good, we shall have not a cosmos but a chaos, not a social order at all but a riot of unrelated individuals. That way lies disaster, not progress.

Nor is it only a matter of unity of theme. To make the truest harmony we must subordinate our playing of the right part to the interest of the whole. Many a chorus made up of good voices fails to produce the true effect because each member wants to be heard

and seen, and will not do his part in the spirit
of teamwork.

There are good pianists who are intolerable
accompanists because they cannot subordinate
their own lesser part to the greater interest of
the vocal score. Is there not a needed lesson
here for all our life? Is not its lack of harmony due largely to our selfishness, our desire to shine, our unwillingness to lose ourselves in the general effect? How few of us
are content to work on in the ranks, filling
in the needed harmony, while others shine as
the stars. Yet for every one who wins recognition there must be many who fail of it,
if the harmony of life is to be realized. We
cannot play in God's great orchestra until
we learn to care more for the general effect
than for our own part in it. How beautifully
the true spirit shines in John the Baptist!
He had been drawing the crowds, standing out
as the leading figure. Then came Jesus, and
John saw his disciples following the new
Leader, the crowds leaving him for Christ.
What were his attitude and spirit? *"He must
increase, but I must decrease." "This my joy
therefore is fulfilled."* He was glad to drop
into the lower place, to play the humbler part,
if God's great melody might thereby be carried on to higher and nobler outworking.

There is one more strong lesson that music teaches about harmonious living—that all must be responsive to the leader. This is the final, the decisive element of harmonious music. Let each know his part well, and each seek the success of all rather than of self, and yet the best result cannot come unless each keeps his eye on the leader, and plays his part as the leader means that he shall. If there is to be unity, some one mind must choose the theme, interpret it, and direct the playing of all. In him, the leader, is the real hope of harmony. This, which is so obviously a condition of harmony in music, is the real condition of harmonious living. *"The eyes of all wait upon thee."* We must look to our one Leader, must let him direct us. *"I am the way, the truth, and the life,"* said Jesus. Only as you take his interpretation of life and obey him, playing your part under his eye, under the inspiration of his leadership, can you make your life a part of God's real harmony.

Sometimes a great composer takes the baton, and himself conducts one of his own works. How eagerly the orchestra responds! How inspiring the effect, for all feel that surely he knows how it should be played.

My friends, it is the composer who is also the director of our life and of the life of our world. God, who made our life, leads us in the living of it if we will let him. What an inspiration to play our little part under his eye, in the sense of his commanding and perfect direction! *"Thy will be done in earth, as it is in heaven"*—that is what we need. Everywhere are strife and friction, misunderstanding and cross purposes, and all through is the consciousness that we are missing the real meaning and beauty of life through our strife and friction and lack of unity. It is our selfish individualism that is the root of the trouble. Men, groups, nations, we *will* play our own part in our own way, and discord must result. What a glorious achievement it would be if some time we should all pause a moment in our mad, self-absorbed playing, and, seeing the Divine Leader standing ready, should follow his beat and fall into rhythm and melody of his great life-theme of love! What music it would make! That is what it means to be a Christian! To do his will, to play our part in his way, not our own. That is what the church is for, to gather a few of us who want to follow his leading, that we may practice together, and learn how to play our parts in unity and harmony as he would have us.

That is the meaning of the League of Na-

tions, and the Pact of Paris, and all earnest
efforts toward co-operation and good will in
the common life of the world. We are trying
to bring that moment when all the instruments shall blend in one great movement, and
out of chaos shall emerge cosmos, in radiant
beauty. We hear and dream much of the new
song that shall be heard in heaven. Then will
come the perfect harmony, we think. But,
beautiful as that dream is, there is something
better and more immediate for which to strive
—to make God's perfect harmony take the
place of earth's present discord. *"Thy will be
done in earth as it is in heaven."* That must
be our prayer and our aim. The angels sang
centuries ago of peace on earth, for the great
Director had come to bring harmony out of
discord. But not all are yet following his
leadership. We still treat him at best as a
mere Guest Conductor. You and I, who believe in him, must set ourselves to play his
theme as he wants it played, and must pray
and work for the harmony that can come only
through obedience to his will. So may we
bring nearer the glorious time when, "from
all who dwell below the skies, shall the Creator's praise arise," "and the whole earth give
back the song, which now the angels sing."

LLOYD CASSEL DOUGLAS was ordained to the Lutheran ministry in 1903, after graduating from Wittenberg College and Hamma Divinity School, both in Springfield, Ohio.

His early pastorates were in North Manchester, Indiana; Lancaster, Ohio; and Washington, D. C. From 1911 to 1915 he was director of religious work at the University of Illinois, leaving that important post to succeed Dr. Carl S. Patton as the pastor of the First Congregational Church of Ann Arbor, Michigan. In 1921 he went to the First Congregational Church of Akron, Ohio, and in 1926 succeeded Doctor Patton in the pulpit of the First Congregational Church of Los Angeles when Doctor Patton joined the faculty of the Chicago Theological Seminary. Doctor Douglas resigned this charge on January 1, 1929, for the pastorate of St. James United Church, Montreal, Canada, and Doctor Patton returned to his former charge in Los Angeles.

Fargo College of North Dakota awarded the D. D. degree in 1920.

His writings are marked by an originality of expression and fearlessness of utterance. Among his books are: *Wanted—a Congregation, The Minister's Everyday Life, These Sayings of Mine, Those Disturbing Miracles.* His helpful orders of service and responsive readings are used by several churches on the Pacific Coast.

Favorite Hymn: "If I have a favorite hymn, it is 'Inspirer and Hearer of Prayer,' to the tune 'Devotion.' "

IV

"HEARTS IN TUNE"

Preached at the Dedication of the Gertrude Mason Raymond Memorial Echo Organ in the First Congregational Church, Akron, Ohio.

Text: O come, let us worship.—*Psalm 95. 6.*

Reduced to its simplest terms, and shorn of all irrelevancies, Religion is the quest of the human soul for an adequate appreciation of its relationship to the divine. Throughout the ages men have pursued this search by devious routes—routes so vastly different that it is not much wonder if one man marvels at his neighbor's ideas on this subject, but the *quest* is ever the same. Our passion to know something about God, our relation to him, our duty to him, and our expectation from him, is the same passion which actuated the sunworshipers, in the remote days of civilization's dawn.

Long before creeds or prophets men searched the skies for heavenly portents, and prostrated themselves in prayer to an Invisible Power. Worship preceded religious cults. Great systems of belief gradually evolved, each owing much, in tradition and sacramenta, to its ancestors and contemporaries. And however we may object to a too lavish ceremonial, the fact remains that a religious system always maintains its integrity as an organization not on a basis of its individuality of belief, but by way of its conservation of an inspirational ritual through which the human imagination may lay hold upon a transcendent idealism.

In our more recent times the church has taken on a wide variety of tasks not previously recognized as component parts of a religious system. It has become conspicuous in the field of altruism and philanthropic service. Its organization composes a veritable network of interlaced committees and auxiliaries, all bent upon the performance of humanitarian duties and the practical display of a gospel of helpfulness.

And this is, of course, a highly commendable program to follow. The religious cultus that contents itself with chanting praises to a transcendent God and intoning pious formulæ traditionally held to be magically potent, while neglecting the active tasks laid upon the souls of all believers, has so missed the point of religion that it would not be too much to say of it that it hasn't any.

In these latter days too heavy emphasis has been placed on the church as a headquarters for altruistic activities; a sort of philanthropic mill, where raw products are worked up into practical benefits for the needy. And where the church does construe her chief function to be as a clearing house for food and clothing, and a sort of branch agency for the collection of money to be spent in building similar institutions elsewhere, she simply takes her place, in the natural scheme of things, alongside all the rest of the organized charities, to the loss of her distinctive commission as a school for spiritual culture.

What the Christian Church, in our day, most seriously stands in need of is a revival of worship. It ought to be a place where tired and jaded people—distracted with the jar and shock and wear and tear of a tumultuous and highly competitive world—can come with the full assurance that they will here find rest unto their souls and a measure of the peace whereby they may rediscover the lost paths to their own hearts.

Religion's first business is to open the way for human-divine contacts through the channels of intellect and the emotions. If through this contact a man becomes impressed with his duty to contribute to the welfare of his world, then the religion he has embraced may be said to have served him well. But religion's primary task is not to show him *how* to serve, but *why.*

Lately, we Protestants have begun to take stock of what we are doing in our churches to improve our present-day civilization. We have just begun to be a bit skeptical of some of the programs of effort on which we had placed our whole reliance. We have begun to fear that we have been putting the cart before the horse, and confusing the cause and the effect, and mistaking certain means for ends.

In our great ecclesiastical conventions for the past score of years the big words have been *service, work,* a *busy* church. The house of God ought to be open twenty-four hours of the day, and working three shifts. Energetic people should be hurrying about within the sacred inclosure, doing rapidly and efficiently a large number of useful things. A favorite motto in populous religious conclaves has been, *"The King's business requireth haste."*

I think we will be gradually coming around to it, in the little group of years now before us, that it is veriest nonsense to believe that *"the King's business requireth haste."* It's mighty little we know about God, but we can be reasonably sure he is not in a hurry. It took him, according to very conservative estimates, about a million years to bring humanity up out of mere brute stupidity and lethargy. The problem of evolving a highly intellectual and wisdom-conserving race is not one that can be solved in a hurry. We had better make up our minds to that and leave off this breathless effort to make the whole world kind and good and happy by *Thursday*.

I do not wish to be misunderstood, at this point, as an advocate of a tranquil selfishness that is willing to let the world go its way with no investment of personal effort toward making it better. I am only calling attention to the fact that there has been too much bustling about in our religious activities, as if we had laid hold of a problem that had to be solved this winter. It's very easy to overstate a commendable duty and overemphasize an important task.

Even the Lord himself was obliged to caution his disciples occasionally when he saw them racing off with some fragment of gospel, mistaking it for the whole of the gospel. There is often a danger in this.

On one occasion an enthusiastic friend, heavily in Jesus' debt, poured a costly vial of perfume over him. At that moment the disciples happened to be completely infatuated

with the new social program of Jesus and considered everything wasted that wasn't practically relieving the unfortunate lot of the poor.
And they chided him for accepting this expen-
sive gift, which, to their thinking, was utterly
squandered.

Said they, "It could have been sold, and the
money given to the poor!"

And Jesus replied: "I shall be with you only
a little while longer. You will have the poor
with you always!"

On another occasion the disciples, enthused
over the prospect that Jesus' moral code, if
believed and practiced generally, would right
all wrongs and usher in a golden age, recom-
mended a drastic application of the new gospel to all cases of social injustice. People
must be made to come to time and either accept the new policy of life or be shown up for
what they were—usurers, extortioners, and
hypocrites.

And then he told them a story of a field of
grain. In that field had been planted wheat.
An enemy had sown tares there too. How, now,
to get rid of the tares?—that was the question. Was it better to go into the growing
grain and pull up the tares, to the ruthless destruction of the wheat? Or was it not good
judgment to wait until harvest and let the

winnowing fan decide what grain was fit to keep and what was destined to blow away?

Nobody ever saw Jesus in a hurry. Nobody ever heard him talk of religion's task as if it were a rush job that had to be put through on contract before the expiration of a certain date.

"If I be lifted up," he said, "I will draw all men unto me"—but he did not say that all this was going to happen as an *act*. He knew it was a *process*.

Now, I am saying these things because they are in line with the newer thinking concerning the real function of the church as an agency of spiritual culture rather than a mill for the volume production of altruistic service. The church is going to achieve more philanthropic results, in the long run, if it provides some spiritual motive for the public, whereby people will wish to project their lives in humanitarian service. Let the church furnish the inspiration!

It is at this point that we have been committing some egregious blunders. Many of our churches appear to have interpreted their errand to be that of a social club, bent on doing a little charity. In their opinion, the church is a sort of rendezvous for a given group who make it their social center and headquarters for whatever they do for their fellow men. We have developed what might be called the folksy type of church, wherein nothing is sacred, nothing is holy, nothing is venerable, and very little is inspirational. Such churches are distinctly secular and of the earth earthy.

In about seven churches out of nine, in our modern American Protestantism, practically nothing ever happens that makes people forget their workaday cares for a little while to seek converse with their own souls. They sit and chatter, through the organ prelude, of matters which may have no relation whatsoever to the church or religion. There are no moments of blessed quiet. There is no chance for meditation. They go in, loaded with concern for the performance of more or less trivial tasks, and come out with the same load, unstirred by any appeal to take reckoning of their own motive power.

The music is of an indifferent order; the ritual has no sequence; the hymns are tawdry examples of poor composition set to worse tunes—sounding like the joint effort of Pollyanna in collaboration with some second-rate jazz-artist.

Not much wonder the people talk all through such a service. Not by the most painful stretch of the imagination could such a performance be listed as a *religious* service.

I have no wish to offer too harsh a criticism of our contemporaneous churches, but the fact is apparent that they are doing almost everything else than the thing which may be considered their primary task. The man who finds himself driven to the wall by his problems and seeks quiet and calm and a fresh grip on the majesty of a divine guidance, these days, had better go out and take a long walk in the woods, along the bank of a river, and try to find God there, than to make the disillusioning adventure of going into some churches, where he cannot hear himself think, for the racket of whispered conversation, which even the nerve-wrenching dissonances of the average organist and the unholy screech of the average choir cannot drown.

For many years this church has made an honest effort to provide a service of worship. We have tried to surround this Sunday-morning service with an atmosphere of peace and quiet. We have discouraged parents from bringing in crying babies and fidgety little people. We have provided a nursery and an excellent kindergarten so that small children could be much better served than if they were brought into this auditorium. We have insisted upon quiet here from the beginning of the organ prelude to the end of the service. Mostly we have been successful. Now and again somebody visits us who has been trained to believe that the organ prelude is a mere accompaniment to idle chatter, but I think we have reduced all such thoughtless sacrilege to a minimum. This has come to be a place where one might expect to find a little tranquillity on Sunday.

And perhaps our success in disposing of the rasping irritations of the chronic whisperer, who makes life wretched for everybody in his (or her) vicinity—at lectures, operas, concerts, and almost any place—is due, in no small measure, to the quality of the music offered here. This choir is entirely consecrated to its task, and it knows what that task is. Its leadership has been fully adequate to inspire it with this motive. So well has it performed its work, and so rewarding has been its labor, that it is known to-day practically throughout the country for the unique service it performs in assisting people to worship.

The new organ enters upon a very significant ministry. It will stir sluggish consciences; it will console the sorrowing; it will energize to active service. It will lift us out of ourselves and encourage us to renew the faith in supernal things which our materialistic age so casually drowns with cynicism. Here, on the Lord's Day, one may come, confident that there will be an opportunity for sobering and steadying meditation, carried forward under the spell of devotional music.

I know of no finer contribution that the church can make in this age of noise and confusion.

Whatever will move upon our moods to the production of harmony between our spirits and the realm of the Ineffable must be regarded a holy thing—consecrated unto the Lord.

GAIUS GLENN ATKINS has been professor of homiletics and sociology in Auburn Theological Seminary, Auburn, New York, since 1927. The titles of his books are mystical reminders of the Unseen. Among his volumes are *Things that Remain, Pilgrims of the Lonely Road, The Undiscovered Country, Craftsmen of the Soul,* and *Modern Religious Cults and Movements.*

An editorial in The Congregationalist of February 7, 1929, pays high tribute to his scholarship and spirit. "It is in itself a form of genius to possess and to exercise a lodestone of faith that discovers everywhere kinships and elements of common life, a passion for fellowship which peoples one's universe with friendly souls."

He was graduated from Ohio State University in 1888, and Cincinnati Law School in 1891, later studying in Yale Divinity School.

His Congregational pastorates have been in Greenfield, Massachusetts; Burlington, Vermont; Detroit, Michigan; and Providence, Rhode Island.

The University of Vermont conferred the Doctor of Divinity degree upon him in 1904, Dartmouth following in 1906. In 1923 the University of Vermont made him a Doctor of Literature.

Favorite Hymn: "Spirit of God, Descend Upon My Heart." "It is noble in conception, finely poetic in expression."

V

THE ORGAN SPEAKS

PREACHED AT THE DEDICATION OF THE ORGAN IN THE FIRST CONGREGATIONAL CHURCH, DETROIT.

Text: And David and all the house of Israel played before the Lord on all manner of instruments.—*2 Samuel 6. 5.*

THIS morning a new and nobly moving voice is heard in this church. Dreams and hopes long entertained have been built into a marvelous combination of pipes and keys and stops and are waiting only the organist's touch to fill all our arched spaces with their harmonies. The dedication of a great organ is so distinctive an event that we may well take the organ itself and its manifold voices for our text, and consider what their meanings are and what their ministry is likely to be through the years.

An adequate organ painstakingly built is, to begin with, the one continuing voice in any church. Ministers and singers come and go, but the organ remains. This organ as we now dedicate it is likely to remain here longer than any member of this morning's congregation.

When our voices have long been stilled, its responsive pipes will support the praise of future generations, taking no hurt from the years, but being instead made more mellow. It will be always waiting the organist's touch; he will have but to press a button, combine his stops, caress his keys, and lo! obedient voices will speak a universal language; they will celebrate our victories for us, hearten us in our defeats, quiet us in our restlessnesses, and bear us out upon their tides to those high regions where the discords of life are resolved in the harmonies of the peace of God.

No other instrument can do so much, so nobly or so continuously. A noble orchestra is the supreme creation of musical genius, but an orchestra is always being made and dissolved. A great organ contains in itself more single elements of power and melody than any one instrument men have ever devised. But an organ has other voices than its pipes, and I shall ask you to listen to it this morning not only for what it says to us as it speaks in its own tone, but for what it says to us as we consider all the elements which have combined to create it and the great art whose ministry it is.

I

Very directly and simply an organ teaches

us that every great achievement is cumulative, being built out of the past and being the creation of no single builder. Every organ began long, long ago and very simply. A Greek poet would have said that this and every other organ began when the great god Pan took a reed from the riverside, pierced and played upon it and awoke therefrom some wild, untutored harmony. The music of these pipes began with the breath of the wind in the reeds, the sounds of the storm in the forest and the diapason of the surf. An organ was only a single pipe to begin with and breath blown. For millenniums the musician contented himself with his reed or his flute and awoke therefrom such harmonies as, in old tales, charmed even inanimate nature. The musician learned next how to make himself a pipe of metal and so to twist and stop it as to make it responsive to the vibrant music of his own spirit.

Far later some one discovered, Saint Cecilia they say, that with a bellows and a wind chest a whole group of pipes could be made to speak at once, and so organ building began. It began, as all great things, very simply. There are organs in France hundreds of years old, with keys hung on wires, which are still speaking and still praising God.

Step by step builders and musicians have

gone on to perfect what began so long ago. They have studied tonal effects, they have added metal to wood, they have called upon vibrating strings and built into their structure tubes and metal plates till you hear bells and harps and haunting lovely tones. They have found new methods of control and bade electricity help them through a most delicate and immediately responsive mechanism. It is possible now to separate pipe and keyboard, to make organ answer to organ across all the spaces of the church, until the music, echoing from quarter to quarter, seems to wash all the walls with its waves.

A great organ is far more than the revelation of the builders' craft; it is also the revelation of the musician's art. These tones in which we rejoice are by no means simple; they are actually built up by adding voice to voice until only a musician could disentangle them. They are ideas, experiences, ideals wrought into unity, and speaking with a sonorous strength.

Every great human achievement is like that —line upon line, precept upon precept, here a little and there a little, until the whole finds a majestic articulation to move us to wonder or to praise. The vast economic mechanism of which we are a part—our laws, our institutions, the entire inter-wrought fabric of our lives—is, like this organ, built through the cumulative wisdom, the laborious endeavor, the questing vision of uncounted generations. What else is our human world but an organ of countless pipes and parts to sound the whole sad, rich music of humanity? The great voices of the poet, of the prophet, or the statesman are always corporate voices. Their overtones are rich in what men have known, or sought, or suffered, or dared. Our achievements have been made possible only through the contribution of fellow craftsmen, the outcome of whose labor continues though they themselves have been forgotten. Any builder may proudly put his name plate upon the organ he has built, but he could never have built it had not the nameless labored with him. We may hear in the tones of an organ the faith, the pity, and the triumph of all lovers of music since music first began.

An organ also teaches us, as life itself teaches us, that it needs a great instrument to voice all the meanings of life. Our world is an organ and so are our souls. Whatever harmony our lives possess is dearly bought and variously created. It needs manifold combinations of wisdom, unselfishness, insight, and power to make any soul rich and vibrant.

The music of our lives, like the music of an
organ, speaks out of the seen and the unseen,
the present and the past, out of forces and
capacities which have been shaped and voiced
by the Master Builder who has created us
through long inheritance and various experience to be the voices of his Spirit. Nothing
which has profoundly affected us is alien to
whatever music our spirits are capable of pro-
ducing. Our sorrows and our happinesses, our
losses and our gains, our repentances and our
sanctities all combine to make the music of
the soul, and time itself has a ripening force
to make that music more mellow.

II

This organ teaches us again how both liberty and law combine to make the music of an
organ and the music of the soul. The laws
which control music are as inexorable as the
laws which control mathematics. All sound
is vibration just as heat and light are vibrations. Light, heat, and sound are the sustain-
ing trinity of life and each is but an impon-
derable tide composed of aerial or ethereal
waves. If there were a way to stop and still
forever the vibratory waves of light, our world
would be lost in darkness. If there were a
way to stop and still the vibratory waves of

heat, all life would perish in an absolute zero. If there were a way to stop and still sound waves, though we spoke to one another, we should make no sound and would live and die in silence.

During the Great War an ingenious writer imagined a master enemy of society as having power to do just these three things—to darken, silence, and freeze the world. If any man had that fancied power, he would hold the fortunes of humanity in his hand.

And music belongs to this trinity; it is sound directed and controlled; its notes are only numbered vibrations and our ears are attuned only to a certain range of them. There is a music too low for us to hear just as there is a music too high for us to hear, and perhaps there are other beings more sensitive than we who acknowledge a harmony to which we are not attuned. The poets have long dreamed of the music of the spheres, as though the stars sung together in choruses we have no power to catch, and science confirms the possibility of these dreams.

A vast deal of the rich variety of music depends upon the material employed to make it. A vibrating wire gives us one tone, a violin string another, a trumpet another still, while the organ pipes have a tone all their own. And yet all these may sing together because they answer the same law of vibration. All instrumental music is built up out of such combinations as these, but the basis of all harmony is harmonic vibration and the mathematical laws which govern this are as rigid as the multiplication table or a proposition in Euclid.

And yet upon this basis of law we build the freest structure in the world. There is no human art which demands so perfect an obedience to so inexorable a law as music. One instrument out of tune and your symphony is no longer a perfect symphony. But there is no human art through which creative freedom has so vast a range as the musician's art. Once the musician accepts the limitations of his art and purchases his perfect freedom with a perfect obedience, he owns a world whose possibilities can never be exhausted. If an organist should sit at the keyboard of an organ for a long eternity, there would still be in its pipes some music still unvoiced. He would find no limitations here but the limitations of his own soul. Musicians have been writing for centuries out of the simple elements of eight accordant tones and if there be no new symphonies to write and new arias to delight us, it is because we are only waiting for other Beethovens and Handels to be born. If heaven is to be a long exercise of praise, as our fathers used to think, it will not be for the want of musical material that their dreams will fail.

This organ will teach you also through the years how every instrument becomes a different instrument beneath the different musicians' touch. The note of the piano is only the response of a wire to a hammer blow, and yet a critic blindfold may tell you whether Hofmann or Paderewski has touched the key. Some difference is in the technique itself, some habit of attack or release; some difference may be in the structure of the hand itself, but the vaster difference is in the temperament and spirit of the musician. Any musical score is only notes on a staff; any organ is only a marvelous device of harmonic and obedient response; music is somewhere else. It is a matter of color and warmth and intellectual conception and emotional passion or restraint. One musician will make a dream of a passage and another will make it a trumpet, and yet each plays from the same score.

More searchingly still, the musician himself is the real instrument. All else from his fingertips to the organ pipes is but the mechanism of the immaterial; unless he be played upon by the music he renders what he does is dead. All great music is twice an interpretation; it is first the composer's interpretation of harmonies to whose insistent realities all are deaf but himself. The composer seizes out of the silence the music which he catches in his curious notations, and, if he be like all the rest of us in the haunting imperfectness of his best endeavor, he hears a music which he can never set to any score at all. The organist in turn becomes the interpreter of the composer, adding elements of his own understanding and feeling which make it live. It is, therefore, in the end life itself which speaks through the organ pipes and moves you to ecstasy or to tears as the violinist plays not upon the strings of his violin, but upon your heart strings.

All great music is both written and played out of some rich understanding of life, which, as we shall see in a moment, can find no adequate voice at all except in music. I should think it true that it needs some hidden wealth of life and many searching experiences to make a musician at all. They seem often enough to belong to a world of their own and do not always happily adjust themselves to our conventional ways, but in the region of their own art they keep faith with the God of music and write and play out of hidden comradeship. A great critic once said of a great singer that she needed only a broken heart to make her a great artist. There is a music that cannot be made articulate except the full organ of life be used, and then, out of his sorrow and his joy, his faith, his hope, his love, his passion and his power, the musician commands, the instrument answers, and our own souls become chambers of echo and response.

III

We are not pressing our illustration, then, too far to say that life itself ought to be lived in the harmonious development of its powers, in the full employment of all its pipes and stops. We are most of us sadly like organs whose keyboards have never known a master musician's touch. No one has ever revealed yet, save the Master of life himself, what music may be evoked from a single life, in what harmonic splendor the enterprises of the soul may be carried through. We reveal at our best but brokenly how nobly duty may be accomplished, how luminous wisdom may become, how graciously friendship may be brought into action, how tenderly love may be made manifest. We reveal at our best but brokenly the grandeur of courage, the vast inclusiveness of faith, the perfection of holy obedience.

Our lives are such inadequate instruments, not because the great chords of them have been lost, but because they have never been found and sounded. From time to time even the commonest life may be so possessed and used as to evoke from it a wonder of beauty and strength we never dreamed that it possessed. It should be our passion and our desire to reveal these unrealized possibilities, to sound these muted notes. We have at our best commonly used so little of ourselves, there is so much discord and so little harmony, so many Misereres and so few Te Deums, so many minors and so few exultant strains. We need a master organist at the keyboards of our lives and there is no touch to awaken all the muted music of the soul like the touch of Jesus Christ with his challenge to courage, his summons to sacrifice, his power to kindle love into flame and his revelation of what lives may truly become.

And if the little organs of our single lives do for the most part reveal so little of what they might make manifest, how much still remains to be sounded in the great organ of humanity! We have as yet evoked with complete success only the disharmonies of society. We have made a thunderous and grandiose music with our guns, but the great organ of human brotherhood has not as yet thrilled us with its diapason. The noblest notes of human well-being are as yet almost unsounded; there is a capacity in our human fellowships which still waits to be brought into action. God pity us that with so noble an instrument we have done so little, and God forgive us the discords which we have offered in the stead of those concords which our fellowships were created to express.

The fault is in ourselves, our acid discontents, our unworthy satisfactions, our slowness of understanding, our self-centerednesses, and our darkened vision. We will not use the instruments we actually possess. There have always been dreamers persuaded that there are ways to order the human enterprise to make a noble music of it and make it the harmony of God's way with men. Industry might become a tremendous instrument of social well-being; it might be made to sound the music of the kingdom of God; the contact of the nations and their international relationships might become the instrument of the noblest harmonies. I think it might be necessary to rebuild many of our social instruments in such fashion as to make them more perfectly responsive to the ideal order, but I think the fault also to be that we do not use what we have in the best way.

If our souls were attuned to the harmonies of the kingdom of God, if we sought to voice the insight and spirit of Jesus Christ in all our affairs, we would discover that what we long for is more largely resident in the circumstance and surroundings of our lives than we dream, and that there is a music even in the imperfect mechanism of society which needs only a proper human touch to fill our world with the glory of it.

And, finally, this organ is here to teach us how the most wonderful things in life can not be put into words at all, but need some universal voice through which emotion and imagination can find an expression to which mere words are unequal. There is, of course, an intellectual element in all music. The trained musician contends that music is first of all an appeal to the intellect, and that unless we try to understand it with our mind we shall do all sorts of foolish things in trying to read our emotions into it; and that is true. And yet music means much because it emancipates the imagination, furnishes a voice to the emotions, releases us from the commonplace, and bears us out upon the mounting tides of it into some ample region of freedom and dreams, where for a little our entranced spirits, carried beyond the bournes of space and time, are at home in the infinite. There we find solace and peace.

It is as if all the tears of things should be caught in the vibration of Kreisler's violin strings and the courage of all the wars be heard in the fanfare of a trumpet. Here is a viewless tide to bear the soul to rapture or to pain.

Music means to us what we make it mean, and it can say nothing to us which is not already in some fashion a part of our own experiences, but under such limitations as these it does for us what nothing else can do. It weaves our hopes, our fears, our dreams, our loves into a magic shimmering web; it sets us free from the stained and unworthy and more than anything else reveals to us what the purely spiritual may be without the taint of earth at all. It is not alone in so serving our highest needs; it shares its ministry with poetry and art with the stars, and the mountains, and the sea, with the magic of twilight and the shadowed coolness of forest spaces, with purple heather upon Devonshire moors as though a cloud had been let down and caught and kept to clothe bare spaces with celestial beauty. Such things as these have their own voice and speak directly to what is deepest within us.

But music, I think, has a quality of its own which nothing else possesses, and supplies for us a sacramental suggestion which is as though the voice of God had been made articulate.

ROBERT ELLIOTT BROWN joined the faculty of Oberlin School of Religion in 1929 after a five-year pastorate in the First Congregational Church, Oakland, the pulpit which Dr. Charles Reynolds Brown made of wide influence for fifteen years in the center of the growing city opposite the Golden Gate.

In his sermon one finds, as one might expect, apt reference to modern science, for Doctor Brown knows scientific literature, and has more than a passing acquaintance with electrons, of which his brother-in-law, Robert A. Millikan, writes so fascinatingly.

A Canadian by birth, he was educated at Oberlin College, of which he is a trustee, and at Yale Divinity School. Carleton College conferred the D. D. degree upon him in 1921.

From 1904 to 1911 he was pastor of the Pilgrim Congregational Church, of New Haven, Connecticut, going to the Second Congregational Church of Waterbury, Connecticut, in 1911, where he remained thirteen years. During the Great War he served in France under the Y. M. C. A.

His lectures on Hymnology in the Pacific School of Religion, Berkeley, California, revealed a vast knowledge and love of the hymns of the church. He is the author of *Christian Certainties*. His verse appears frequently in the local press.

Favorite Hymn: "Lord of All Being, Throned Afar."

THE ROAD OF THE LOVING HEART

By Robert Elliott Brown

Tune: *St. Peter's,* Oxford

Lord, send me forth upon that road
   My feet be swift to go,
Where I may bear a brother's load
   And share another's woe.

Perchance upon that way I'll find
   Some soul whom foes oppress,
Whose bleeding wounds are mine to bind,
   Whose spirit I may bless.

Instill my heart with pity, Lord,
   To lessen pain and grief,
And grant me skill to work thy will
   Providing sweet relief.

Thus may I walk with open heart
   Inspired by love for thee,
And know that strength to do my part
   My recompense shall be.

VI

THE HARMONY OF RELIGION

Text: "Thou shalt meet a band of prophets coming down from the high place with a psaltery, and a timbrel, and a pipe, and a harp, before them; and they shall be prophesying."—*1 Sam. 10. 5.*

To many people religion seems like a bedlam of sounds. It is an orchestra sadly out of tune. Either the instruments cannot or will not play together. The followers of religion must often give the appearance of musicians forever sawing and scraping, but never performing a masterpiece unitedly and effectively. The various sects of religion often seem to make for discord rather than concord. Strange and harsh-sounding doctrines break up the sweet melody that religion is expected to produce.

One must in all honesty admit that in reading the history of religion even down to the present time there is much to justify such a point of view. Sects, schisms, persecutions, and dissensions have marked religion as a riot rather than a rhythm, a scrimmage rather than a symphony.

But here we have the basis for the opposite suggestion. We see a band of prophets coming down from the high place, that is, from a high hill where people met for worship and sacrifice. They are playing upon the psaltery, timbrel, pipe, and harp. Each instrument has its true place with respect to all the other instruments. The music they make is a reflection of a harmony they feel within their own souls. The same inner harmony enabled them to worship in singleness of spirit, and it sent them forth to prophesy in the name of the Lord with fullness and with power.

These men could not have lived together companionably, nor have worshiped congenially, nor have piped melodiously, nor have prophesied effectively unless they had first been inspired by the humanizing power of religion.

And so it is with the church to-day. It will not worship with joy nor prophesy with power unless it secure a harmony within itself that shall satisfy the mind and heart and soul and give to the world something of God's music which the world by itself can never obtain.

A great orchestra represents the evolution of three thousand years. It is the embodiment of the history, science, and art of music. It has gathered the musical experience of civiliza-

tions that we call Semitic, Greek, Roman, and
Modern. Man's highest moods and hopes and
feelings are the moving spirits behind each
instrument and immanent in each performer.
To express the widest range of ideas, to do
justice to each emotion and to incite to the
noblest action, experience discovered and dis-
closed not a single instrument, but whole fami-
lies of instruments. As a church represents
households desirous of a common expression
of religion, and anxious for a mutual exchange
of feelings, and determined to give a co-ordinated message to a community, so an orchestra
evolved instruments—wood, brass, and strings
—to give every possible shade and timbre of
tone in an attempt to express the infinite in-
audible harmonies of the universe.

The outstanding motive of religion is harmony. It can unite men as it united these
prophets, and as it held together men of every
tribe at Pentecost. It is only by religion that
we can hold together elements of thought and
experience that seem discordant and contra-
dictory. Birth, life, death, work, pain, sorrow,
hope, despair—these are either the greatest
jangle of warring sounds or they are the notes
of the most stupendous symphony that the
mind of God could compose. Which they shall
be for us will depend upon whether we ally

ourselves with the prophets or with the pessi-
mists.

In the story we see men representing a
primitive culture. Life is simple. Thought is
unscientific. The world is a miniature in extent and religion is naïve. Yet they had found
the higher harmonies of the spirit. God was
near and certain and precious. That was the
essence of their experience.

To-day our life is complex. Thought is
critical. The world is large. The universe is
infinite. Religion itself is often apologetic and
discordant and hesitant. The question for us
is this, Can we find the higher harmonies of
the spirit as these men felt them? Has our
boasted progress come to mean the loss of faith
and emphasis upon the discords of existence?

Let us ascend into the high place of the
spirit and realize that religion has the harmony of life to offer us and that we may find
joy, faith, unity, and power as truly as did this
band of men who went forth to proclaim the
presence and power of God. Let us analyze
and describe this Harmony of Religion.

In the first place the religion of to-day must
proclaim the note of intelligence, and this on
the undeniable experience of the race.

Twenty-four hundred years ago Anaxagoras
arose in Greece and declared that mind per-

vades the universe. "Sometimes," he said, "mind is parallel with matter, as distinct from matter as a player is distinct from his violin." Sometimes he maintained that mind permeated matter as the wind permeates the mechanism of a stately organ. But Anaxagoras was ahead of his time. His doctrine seemed to rob the gods of their power when it was well known that they lived and ruled on Mount Olympus! Anaxagoras was denounced for his heresy and was sent into exile. He was as far ahead of his generation as was Wagner, who after performing his new and matchless creations in Paris was hissed off the stage.

In the eighteenth century Hegel arose in Germany and declared the world to be rational. He saw an order and a sequence that led him to maintain that absolute mind infuses all reality. He suffered no exile nor even an inconvenience. The intervening centuries between him and Anaxagoras had prepared the world for this note in the orchestration of thought, until to-day who will not join in the chorus,

> "To see a world in a grain of sand,
>   And heaven in a flower,
>   To hold infinity in the palm of the hand,
>   Eternity in an hour"?

The complexities of the material universe are

compressed into a grain of sand. The artistry
of all creation is in a single rose. The thought
of God is stamped on every human face and
the heart of God is inherent in every child.

Hegel felt that the intelligence of the Divine
Mind permeated the whole universe just as
Wagner felt that the infinite harmonies of an
invisible creation were sounding in his ear.

It is of interest to note to-day how this doctrine that the world is rational is being
preached in the most surprising manner. Psy-
chologists are no longer saying that instinct
alone rules in the animal world. They demand
that intelligence be assigned to that domain.
On one of Peary's voyages to the pole he and
his men were beaten back to their base, having lost, as they believed, every dog in their
pack. But they were mistaken. One dog sur-
vived the terrible ordeal of border-line starva-
tion. He came back to camp and slowly re-
vived. But for days he hid a portion of his
food, as if the lesson of providing for the
future had been evolved from his terrible experience with hunger and danger.

Science is not driving intelligence out of the
universe. It is bringing it back with such a
fanfare as to make the materialists weep with
disappointment. The biologist finds that even
the cell acts as if by the power of mind. The

physicists assert that the atom is a solar system in miniature. If the heavens show the handiwork of God, then the electrons are the work of his fingers. When Sir Michael Costa was once directing his great orchestra in London it is said that, amid the crash and fury of the instruments, he stopped the whole performance and demanded, "Where is the piccolo?" It was a testimony that the smallest element in the orchestra incorporated within itself something of the harmonious powers of the whole ensemble. Science is not driving intelligence out of the universe. It is, rather, challenging religion to measure up to a universe that is pregnant with mind and gives every evidence of being the work of God.

At first sight we might say music is entirely æsthetic creation. But that would not be true. A modern orchestra, by reason of its variety of instruments, its laws of harmony, its composition of tones and its co-ordination of effort, is an outstanding triumph of the human intelligence. Great composers are regarded as mental geniuses, and so if there is a rationality in music, we believe there is a rationality in religion and in life. We will surrender no human problem to indifference or despair. But permeating the industrial and social and international and interracial perplexities is the power of mind, and we will hold to the belief that as we find the truth we shall also find the way that leads to right and justice.

In the second place, religion is humanistic. Rationality cannot exhaust religion any more than the flute family can claim all the orchestra. Man has never been willing to sit by and simply think out the harmony of existence. He has ever been aroused by the bugle call of humanism as it sounded over the hills of Galilee nineteen hundred years ago, and as it reverberates through every city when the silver trumpet of sacrifice is sounded for the community chest. Once there was a boy who was asked in history class who Nero was. His answer was, "The man who played the fiddle when he should have played the hose."

In the orchestra of life there is a place for speculation, but not to the detriment of salvation. John Burroughs discloses the gospel of humanism in affirming the faith of a naturalist. He says: "We need not fear alienation from God. I feed him when I feed a beggar. I serve him when I serve my neighbor. I love him when I love my friend. I praise him when I praise the wise and good of any race or time. I shun him when I shun the leper. I forgive him when I forgive my enemies. I wound him when I wound a human being. I forget him when I forget my duty to others. If I am cruel or unjust or resentful or envious or inhospitable toward any man or child, I am guilty of all these things toward God." "Inasmuch as ye have done it unto one of the least of these my brethren, ye have done it unto me." This is only the extension of the scripture, *"He that loveth not his brother whom he hath seen, how can he love God whom he hath not seen?"*

The inevitable trend of progress is toward humanism. Education, art, science, and medicine are tending to carry their blessings down to the lowest and out to the farthest. Religion cannot do otherwise. So to-day it is penetrating the remotest places by the most progressive methods. It is said that the radio will revolutionize the country church, bringing it music and preaching that it has not heretofore been able to obtain. Religious books are circulating as never before by means of the parcel post, and increasingly bus lines will gather up the children for religious instruction at convenient locations. And with this there will be an intensive effort to bring the comfort of religion to souls that are truly in need. It was the strongly individualistic Emerson who made the confession, "What I

need is someone to keep me at my best." That
is the universal experience. We are too likely
to think that all human needs are met by education, food, shelter, clothing, and medical
care, but companionship is as fundamental to
the soul as medical aid is to the body. Religion without love is like an orchestra when
only the cymbals clang and the drums roll.
They may beat out the rhythm by which we
are to march, but that is all. They cannot
give us the melody of friendship which stirs
the heart. There is nothing like rationalism
to tone up the mind and tune up all the inherent intelligence. God save us from the igno-
rance and jazz of superficial thinking! There
is nothing like humanism to enrich the heart.
It is the very breath of Jehovah, creating the
melody of existence. Theology has not perfectly unified these two elements. Neither has
philosophy. It has too often been a solo
played in isolation from the world or a wail in
the desert when it should have been a festival
in the fields, or it has been chamber music for
the élite when it should have been a Hallelujah Chorus in the market place.

If the history of human thought tells us anything, it is that intelligence severed from the
problems thrust upon us by nature and the
vital interests of humanity are a waste of

energy and a threat of destruction to the powers of the mind itself. The rules of existence apply to the reason as to every other faculty in the soul. Reason comes to its best inheritance when it serves to direct and inspire the forces that make for the harmony and enrichment of life.

And religion is spiritual as well as rational and human, for there will ever be needed the note of mysticism. It takes these three to strike the full chord of the heavenly music.

Those prophets in the story went forth to prophesy in the name of a God whom they could not see as one player sees another and whose voice they could not hear as we hear a record on a phonograph. But they could apprehend him by faith. They could feel him by the power of intuition. They could conceive him by the projecting power of their reason. He was real and present to them.

The doctrine of spirituality to-day is sounded forth not from the pulpit alone. There are prophets in the high places of science affirming a belief in the reality of the soul. Sir William Bragg, president of the British Association for the Advancement of Science, has recently said, "Science is not so foolish as to throw away that in which the slowly gathered wisdom of the ages is stored."

The soul is a miniature of the cosmos, and is stored with its truth and spirit.

Once we admit the existence of a soul in man, we are open to the belief that soul forces permeate the universe.

It was Monteverde in the eighteenth century who demonstrated the necessity of stringed instruments to provide the foundation elements of a modern orchestra. There are a passion, a freedom, a mystery and a magic awakened by the strings that are equaled by no other orchestral power. They carry us, as it were, beyond the domain of time and sense, and on the wings of rhapsody they take us to the very gates of paradise. How easily a great symphony gives us the power to affirm,

> "Forever I am conscious, moving here,
> That should I step a little space aside,
> I pass a boundary of some glorified, invisible
> Domain, it lies so near."

Mysticism is to life what stringed music is to the orchestra. In England to-day there is a passionate yearning for a demonstration and proof of God, and so seven hundred and thirty churches of the Anglican faith are turning to Rome in the belief that in the mass there is the one incontrovertible assurance of the Divine Presence. They hold to the teaching that when the priest says a prayer and rings a bell the bread of the communion table is turned into the flesh of Jesus and the wine in the flagon is turned into his very blood. Thus men grown weary with a spiritual faith turn to magic, occultism, and tradition.

It is not for us to stand by and berate and ridicule. We have to ask ourselves, What have we to offer in exchange for such a conception? The words for such a doctrine are found in the Gospel according to John. That we cannot deny. But here, as in so many other places in Scripture, the letter killeth, only the spirit maketh alive. The religion of the spirit will fasten upon another text which is infinitely truer, we believe, to the mind and heart of Jesus. *"The wind bloweth where it listeth, and thou hearest the sound thereof, but canst not tell whence it cometh, and whither it goeth; so is every one that is born of the Spirit."* Religion is the music of God borne on the wings of the Spirit to the eager listening soul of man.

Jesus found the harmonizing power of the Spirit in no single instrument of God's creation. He found God in the rhythmic procession of sunrise and sunset, in the symphony of color that clothed the grass and painted the lily, in the notes of the moral conscience that sounded clear above the confusion and selfishness of the world and in the ever resounding strain of conviction. *"God is a Spirit: and they that worship him must worship him in spirit and in truth."* How paltry seem the claims of magic as they are measured with the message of Him who thought intelligently and served consistently and was conscious of moving always harmoniously and everywhere in the presence and power of God!

LYNN HAROLD HOUGH has the chair of homiletics in Drew University. He was pastor of the American Presbyterian Church of Montreal, Canada, from February, 1928, to September, 1930. Ordained to the Methodist Episcopal ministry in 1898, he has served a number of prominent Methodist Episcopal churches, the last being in Detroit, Michigan.

He is well known as an author and lecturer. Among the books that have come from his pen are: *The Theology of a Preacher, Evangelical Humanism, Imperishable Dreams, The Artist and the Critic.* In 1918 he was sent to Great Britain to speak on the moral and spiritual aims of the war, by the Lindgren foundation of Northwestern University.

He is a popular preacher in England. In The City Temple Pulpit and Church Tidings for September, 1926, we are told that "he straightway won the warm regard and admiration of a congregation not slow to recognize the unmistakable quality of an authentic message. The series of sermons very effectively demonstrated that a message for the world to-day need lose nothing of powerful evangelical appeal because it is broad, based upon conceptions which do not make intellectual death the condition of spiritual life." Dr. J. Fort Newton has paid tribute to his mastery of "a limpid, vivid, musical style—delicate without being dainty, flexible and forthright, rich in color cadence," as well as to "his clear insight and wise guidance in those pathways by which groping man finds his way to the Eternal amid the fogs and illusions of time."

Favorite Hymn: "My God, I Thank Thee."

VII

"WHEN MUSIC GIVES A SOUL TO WORDS"

Text: Praise him with stringed instruments and
     the pipe.
    Praise him upon the loud cymbals:
    Praise him upon the high sounding cym-
     bals.—*Psalm 150. 4, 5.*

WORDS themselves are glorious things. They
are full of secret places where wonderful
meanings are kept.

The Old Testament people produced great
artists in the use of words. Innocent of sculpture and painting, they put a passionate love
of beauty into majestic and sonorous words.
It was with words that they painted pictures.
It was with words that they carved statues.
All their pent-up activity found expression in
melodious and lyrical speech. But even they
felt the need of music in worship. And words
themselves sang with new rhythm as they described the ministry of music.

Praise him with stringed instruments and the
    pipe.
Praise him upon the loud cymbals:
Praise him upon the high sounding cymbals.

103

They felt keenly enough that there were sounds which entered regions from which words were shut out, and on wings of music they rose to regions which words alone could not reach.

Sir Arthur Quiller-Couch closes the fourth lecture on Milton in his *Studies in Literature* with these words: "That is how I see Milton, and that is the portrait I would leave with you —of an old man, lonely and musical, seated at his chamber organ, sliding upon the keyboard a pair of hands pale as its ivory in the twilight of a shabby lodging of which the shabbiness and the gloom molest not him; for he is blind—and yet he sees."

Once and again Milton himself put his passion for music into lofty and harmonious words, as when he speaks of:

"That undisturbed song of pure concent,
  Ay sung before the sapphire-colored throne,
  To Him that sits thereon,
  With saintly shout and solemn Jubily,
  Where the bright Seraphim in burning row
  Their loud uplifted Angel trumpets blow,
  And the Cherubick host in thousand quires
  Touch their immortal Harps of golden wires,
  With those just Spirits that wear victorious
    Palms
  Hymns devout, and holy Psalms
  Singing everlastingly."

Here the words themselves are lifted to new and rapturous meaning by the music whose sweetness has the power of wings. And in less celestial worship than that which Milton describes we have all felt the same strange and beautiful thing to happen. Words have a far reach. But there are tremendous regions beyond. And music carries words to far places where they could never go alone.

The curious fact about words is that they are all the while being drawn by various forces. Sometimes they are pulled down from below. Sometimes they are lifted from above. The tantalizing thing about a stately volume like an unabridged dictionary is just that it is not static. It is dynamic. Words are on the march. Sometimes they drearily go to dull and colorless regions. Sometimes they triumphantly rise to regions of rare and radiant beauty. And words, like armies, march best to the accompaniment of martial music. An old dull word often rises with a new light in its eye when music calls forth its inner vitality like a battle-horn bearing the sharp, clear sound which has once sent it forth upon the charge.

Most Christians are unconscious Platonists. They know that the here and the now find their real and abiding meaning as they are shot through by some sudden light which comes from eternity. So words are real only as some eternal meaning shines through them and makes them incandescent. And music will ignite a candle in every word of a rhyming sentence until it glows like a series of shining lights. So music gives a soul to words.

Our very ritual of worship is like a forest in winter. The trunk is strong. The branches have a certain grace of line, a certain symmetry and cold beauty of their own. But the whole forest waits the call of the springtime, the curious adventure of the green leaves, the shy peeping forth of the buds, and all the abandon and energy of the full blown, when every tree surrenders to the magic of its flowering time. Music will do to a serene and stately ritual, cold and noble, what springtime does to the cold symmetry of winter's forest. And so it edges human experience with the grace of understanding song. And so it captures human hopes like a piece of sculpture which has turned an aspiration into marble. And so it sounds the full grandeur of eternal sanctions. And so it rises to that solemn height when it is full of the sense of God.

The great things of life are infinitely elusive and furtive. We place our hands upon them and they are gone. We make a home for them in our hearts and they vanish away. But music captures them and gives back to us things which seemed too lovely and too fragile for this hard and difficult world.

During the conflagration which hurried all about the world from 1914 to 1918 Arthur Benson published a volume of essays with the significant title *Escape.* The world of high explosives tragically in action was a world from which men might easily wish to find a moment's respite in some land of the mind, where healing silences stilled the heart into the quiet of their own deep peace. Music is often just that which the title of Mr. Benson's volume of essays suggested. It is an escape. And there are times when worship itself made tender and alluring by lovely harmonies may well offer escape to tired spirits worn by the difficult business of living in this demanding and oppressive world. *"Oh for a lodge in some vast wilderness!"* we cry and for a little while we may find escape in the gentle serenities of lovely worship. But escape is a dangerous thing. For it may mean evasion. It may mean the slipping off of the armor of responsibility. It may mean the great refusal to do battle in the high hour. It may mean a lotus-eating lassitude which unfits us for action and the hour of strong endeavor. So the mood of escape must not last too long. The music itself must change from its brooding quiet and its gentle and gracious serenity.

The trumpets must sound and the music which was an escape must become a battle cry.

Some of the greatest music which sings in the heart of our hymns has just this inspiring quality. It is as if one stanza offered us a helmet. Another stanza offered us a sword. And at last all equipped we go forth to the fight with the hymn giving us a heart of courage as it has given us a weapon and a coat of mail.

There is no great sanction in the Christian religion but has received new power to seize the imagination, to master the mind, to dominate the will, to release the strong hand of action, through the subtle potency of music. From the terrible anguish of "He was despised, and rejected of men; a man of sorrows, and acquainted with grief," to the overwhelming victorious shout of the Hallelujah Chorus, the Christian religion has swept into the hearts of men on the wings of song. And the organ has given voice to inexpressible reaches of the spirit of man.

Beyond the music lies the call of life. Beyond the worship wait the responsibilities of the hour. The dilettante listens with ravished spirit to the music, but shrinks from the strain and contentions of the hour of action. The true man lifts the music as a cup with which he pledges his allegiance and goes forth to the fight. There may be shrinking in all our hearts. But we know what hero we would like to follow.

"The Son of God goes forth to war" against sordid selfishness, and hard bigotry, and blighting poverty, and hard tyranny, and the complacency which substitutes the liberal word for the liberal deed, and we would like to follow in his train.

Robert Freeman is the versatile pastor of the Pasadena Presbyterian Church, which stands fifth in the Presbyterian denomination with a membership of 3,364. He has written several hymns, some of which are included in his book of poetry, *The Land I Live In*. Music is one of his recreations. Occasionally he will be found playing the tower chimes in his church. The church owns its own broadcasting apparatus. Many throughout southern California listen to the inspiring sermons and uplifting music of his services.

Coming to America from Edinburgh in 1896 at the age of eighteen, he studied in Alleghany College. Bruce Barton, in an article in The American Magazine, has related the hardships of his early life. He was ordained to the Baptist ministry in 1900, after home missionary service in Pennsylvania and New York. While still studying in Princeton Theological Seminary he journeyed each week-end to Buffalo to preach in the Lafayette Presbyterian Church, where, after his graduation in 1907, he remained for three years as pastor. Coming to California in 1911, he speedily assumed a place of leadership in church life. He was elected moderator of the Synod and for several years has been president of the Board of Trustees of Occidental College. He was director of religious work in France for the Y. M. C. A.

"He is now as much an integral part of Pasadena as the recently erected City Hall," to quote from the Homiletic Review's "Studies of the American Pulpit," where high praise is paid to his Sunday school of almost three thousand pupils, and the missionary spirit of his great church. He has published two devotional books, and a recent volume of sermons entitled *What About the Twelve?*

Favorite Hymn: "O Love That Wilt Not Let Me Go"—"partly because of the hymn and the fitting marriage to a suited tune, and largely because the author was a blind Scotsman whom I myself have heard once and seen many times."

HYMN OF PRAISE

By Robert Freeman

Tune, *Austrian Hymn*

For thy mercy aye pursuing
    Through the winding way of years;
For thy grace our souls enduing
    'Gainst the tumult of our fears;
For thy patience with our crudeness,
    Thy forgiveness toward our ways,
Hear, O hear us, God of Goodness,
    Hear in heaven thy children praise.

For the stars eternal weaving
    In thy loom of everywhere,
For the glory of perceiving
    Suns and dewdrops in thy care;
For a singing heart at duty,
    For the sunset harmonies,
Hear, O hear us, God of Beauty,
    Hear in heaven thy children praise.

For the order of creation,
    Law in earth, in air, and sea;
For the ever sure foundation,
    Universal verity;
For the tides that ne'er betray thee,
    Dawns that never fail the days,
Hear, O God of Truth, we pray thee,
    Hear in heaven thy children praise.

For thy mercy aye pursuing,
  For thy graces ever sure,
For thy goodness ever wooing,
  For thy love that doth endure;
What the wonders of creation?
  What the ages' memories?
God of Love, for our salvation
  Hear in heaven thy children praise.

VIII

"A VIOLIN SERMON"

Text: Making melody in your heart to the
Lord.—*Eph. 5. 19.*

MANY a schoolboy has pasted in his text-
books the printed motto: *"Sine libris vita
mors est,"* "Without books life is death"; and
many more of us have written in our hearts
the motto, *"Sine musica vita mors est,"* for
without music life would be one grand mis-
take—it would be death. But as things are,
there is music everywhere and in everything.
The Egyptian philosophers made it the symbol of the universe; Plato and Aristotle saw in
it the best expression of life; for Pythagoras
the basal principle of philosophy was that God
had organized all nature according to the laws
of harmony.

> "From harmony, heavenly harmony,
> The universal frame began;
> When nature underneath a heap
> Of jarring atoms lay."

> "God is its author and not man; he laid
> The keynote of all harmonies; he planned
> All perfect combinations, and he made
> Us so that we could hear and understand."

Everything in nature is keyed to take its part in the great cosmic symphony. The rolling sands give forth varying sounds: in Hawaii, a barking; on our coast, a higher, thinner note. "Everything the sun shines upon," says Horace Bushnell, "sings, or can be made to sing, and can be heard to sing." Light and sound are alike; flames have modulated voices. The stars of the morning sing together.

"There's not the smallest orb which thou behold'st
But in his motion like an angel sings,
Still quiring to the young-eyed cherubims."

Animate nature too is full of music, and the poet is kept busy taking down the scores she dictates.

"The mocking bird, wildest of singers,
Swinging aloft on a willow-sprig that hung o'er the waters,
Shook from his little throat such floods of delirious music
That the whole air and the woods and the waves seemed silent to listen."

Again Longfellow speaks of the birds,

"Whose household words are songs in many keys,
Sweeter than instrument of man e'er caught;
Whose habitations in the treetops even
Are half-way houses on the way to heaven."

Indeed it is true:

"Music in all growing things;
  And, underneath the silky wings
      Of smallest insect, there is stirred
      A pulse of air that must be heard;
Earth's silence lives, and throbs, and sings."

To the scientist music is only a modification by art of aerial vibrations, whose impact upon the auditory nerve makes mental varying images. But that means but little to most of us. Here is a definition from Carlyle that appeals: "Music is a kind of inarticulate, unfathomable speech which leads us to the edge of the infinite and lets us for a moment gaze into that."

Now, is it not strange that, in such a world as ours, a world whose swaddling clothes were garments of light, a world that daily bathes in rivers of music, and plays its part in the orchestra of the spheres, that in such a world there should be those who having ears to hear hear not, to whom music is only noises, and harmony nothing but discord? But there are such. David Hume, the Scotch philosopher; Doctor Johnson, Sir Walter Scott, Sir Robert Peel, and Lord Byron—none of these had any ear for music; and to such as the poet Samuel Rogers, music gave actual discomfort.

A former professor in Princeton expressed himself as hopeful that he and his dog might live in a cottage in the suburbs of heaven far from the "madding crowd" of harpists and singers.

To the majority of us, however, the musical figure appeals. We are sensible that we are instruments from whom issue sounds more or less pleasing. We are no mere hurdy-gurdies, out of which music can be ground by the pennyworth, but are delicately stringed instruments carefully to be tuned and skillfully to be played upon. The figure of the violin suggests itself to me, though the harp might more nearly describe many whom I know and admire—the violin with its four strings representing four great departments of the common life of man, each string necessary to the instrument, but each string useless or worse unless tuned to an accepted standard and kept in relation to the other three.

There is, first, the deep bass G string of work. The obligation to work is a law of God. He who carefully proscribed work on one day in the week was as careful in the Decalogue to prescribe work on six days of each week. *"I must work"* was one of the mottoes of the life of Jesus. No one who is not willing fairly to

contribute by work to the world's wealth,
whatever his contribution may be, whether by
creation, distribution, or inspiration, has any
right to live and to expect support from society. Labor is a law of life. No legacy justi-
fies leisure. No income exculpates one for
failure to show an output. Any man can earn
a rest, but no man can inherit one. "I must
work" is God's own law for himself. Surely,
he is rich enough to quit, for the silver and the
gold are his, and the cattle on a thousand
hills!

Even where there is not the pressing objective necessity of earning a living, there is the
subjective necessity of personal development.
Some years ago, with three companions and
a guide, I set out at dawn to climb one of the
lofty peaks of the Rocky Mountains. There
was only one horse available, and that was put
at the service of him who had been somewhat
upset by the elevation of some seven thousand
five hundred feet where our camp was. The
bowlder field above timber line ended the service of that lone animal, and the addition of
four thousand feet proved too much for our
semisick companion. The host of our party
felt that the demands of hospitality summoned
him to retreat with his incapacitated guest.
The two who were left found the common ob-

stacles of the most dangerous part of the climb
suddenly and unexpectedly re-enforced by a
storm. The narrows beyond the keyhole on
Long's Peak are dangerous enough anyhow,
but when it rains and freezes at once so that
one's footing is continually precarious, and
one's hands are numb, the risks are greatly
multiplied. Then, the third member of the
quartet of amateur mountaineers was taken ill
and I was too youthful to turn a deaf ear to
his urging that I go on to the top. I wanted
to get there, especially since the conditions
were so adverse. Since then I have made that
climb at other times when conditions were
perfect, but that day it was no child's play.
However, at length, up over the precipitous
slide we made the peak and prostrated ourselves to gasp for breath. Then, for the view!
The guide had told me that from that elevation of fourteen thousand two hundred and
seventy feet one could see a hundred miles in
any direction, and I had conjured up pictures
of the great reaches extending into the neigh-
boring States. But did I see the far ranges of
the lower mountains, or the wide stretches of
waving grain, or "the hell-colored smoke of the
factories" rising from the manufacturing centers below? I could not see my own hand held
up before my face. We were wrapped in fog,

and I was cheated of the reward for which I had labored. And yet, was I? Did I not have the supreme subjective reward of having battled with the elements and having won? I had beat my body under. I had conquered the weakening inclination within and the baffling circumstances without, and I descended supremely satisfied. Work gives us that. Work is the great personal development. *"Establish thou the work of our hands?"* No, that's not all of it. The psalmist does not ask that his creations last forever. *"Establish thou the work of our hands* UPON US.*"* The habit of sloth is disastrous to mind and body; but work, whatever be the tools or materials, is making the workman. God has linked happiness with duty and health with labor. *"My meat is to do . . ."*

This string, then, must be tuned. There is no melody issuing from the heart of the slacker and the loafer, no development for the parasite who is unfortunate enough to have his sustenance provided without his personal effort. "Produce! Produce!" cried Carlyle. "In God's name produce, though it be but the pitifulest, infinitesimal fraction of a product."

Second, there is the mellow D string; that I think of as the symbol of pleasure. There can be no doubt that there is such a string on life's instrument. All work and no play makes Jack a dull boy. The only problem is that of tuning this indispensable string. When is the string of pleasure in tune? is the question with which we who are teachers are continually faced. The youth, sometimes, and the mature who watch over youth, come more frequently with problems of the legitimacy and advisability of this form of recreation and that.

We know that pleasure contributes, as does labor, to the development of the individual character. Perhaps it makes a greater contribution since the teacher is much more beloved. In the field of grain both ridge and furrow help determine the crop. The six-inch drill and the six-foot drill may equally impoverish the harvest. The youth is not sent to college for athletics or dramatics or forensics—these are subordinate. When fraternity parties and class fights and intercollegiate games assume primary consideration, then the player has lost sight of the goal and is traveling across the field; when pleasures become a necessity, they cease to be of value and become, instead, the enemies of the soul. You never hear a solo played on the D string— there are more important strings on each side

of it. Pleasures are only incidental trip ham-
mers in the framing of an ironclad of character. The ultimate, and not the immediate, is
the consideration—not a single note, but a
whole concerto. Pleasures must pull toward
perfection. If in this they fail, in this they
condemn themselves.

Again, there is the A string of friendship
running up and down the scale of our affec-
tions from casual acquaintances up to that in-
comparable experience to be envied by all and
known to most when two lives merge into one,
pledged until death.

The A string is probably more played upon
than any other. Its brilliant notes are continually interwoven whether the composition
seek the higher or the lower ranges. It is the
mezzo-soprano of the instrument. It is the
string by which all the others are tuned; if it
is out of tune, all is out of tune.

I envy for all of you the richest experiences
of human love, the joy of unsullied and unwavering admiration and affection yielded by
that one whose regard is your chiefest desire.
But there will be no such unless the string of
love be in tune. Impurity, irregularity, faith-
lessness, habitual selfishness when the strings
are yet in the tuning will wreck the whole
symphony; while little acts of self-denial and

habitual kindness will train for a life of melody.

The fourth string gives us our highest notes, notes that penetrate to the heart like the song of the nightingale. It is the E string of religion. There they are—love of work, love of pleasure, love of friends, love of God. I am not urging my personal religious convictions upon you, but I am urging the necessity of the religious life. Worship is an art. Religion is a life, it is the life of God in the human soul, the life that continually takes God into consideration. Neglect this string, and you are cut off from all the higher reaches of which your instrument is capable. Let it remain untuned to the great spiritual standards, and you become the discordant note while others swell together in a diapason of faith, hope, and victory. Religion is as necessary to life as work and play and love. Without religion all the other cultivations of life but cry for the lost chord. Religion is the crown and glory of the hardest worker, the gayest player, the most devoted lover.

John Philip Sousa, in a weird tale called "The Fifth String," tells of a Tuscan virtuoso named Angelo Diotti, who played upon a violin with an additional string made up of the extra lengths of the other four woven together.

The fifth string was forbidden to the artist. All his playing must dodge about it without the silken bow's ever falling upon it. The penalty of failure or disobedience was death. We too have a fifth string. As Diotti must not play upon his, so we cannot play upon ours. As his was the string of death, so ours is the string of suffering. It too gathers up all the ends of the other strings, and what they are determines whether music and sweetness or discord and harshness shall issue forth from this string. For it has no key by which to screw up to pitch, and only when work and play and love and worship are in tune can tuneful notes come from suffering. One was made perfect by suffering, and for that end does it come to us all. It is friction that tells the tale. Rubbing and pulling and snapping discovers what is in the violin. It is rosin that the bow needs, not oil. Similarly, the frictions of life, the petty inconveniences and the great trials make audible the melody or discord of the heart. It is not the calm ease of an hour in church on a Sunday, but the pressure and the inconveniences and the irking personalities about us on Monday that discover what is in us.

One may readily fancy the plea of many here: "Mine is such a poor second-rate thing of a life that there is little music to be got out of me." Yet Paganini, when his own instrument had been taken, faced the crowd with a cheap substitute in his hands, saying, "I will show you that the music is not in the violin, but in Paganini himself." Mozart composed his immortal "Requiem" on a broken-down spinet in a garret in Vienna. A master can play on anything; your Master can. So go forth praying God to help you tune the strings devoted to your labor, your leisure, your love, and your Lord, to work, play, friendship, and worship; and praying God too himself so to play upon those strings that you shall know the joy of a melodious heart, and the world shall be glad for your music; himself to play till the last string breaks its quivering strands and the instrument is ready for the new strings and for an honorable place in the greater orchestra.

ALEXANDER MacCOLL, minister since 1911 of the Second Presbyterian Church of Philadelphia, was born in Glasgow, Scotland, coming to the United States in 1886. For five years he edited the Evening Journal, of New Bedford, Massachusetts.

After studying in Union Theological Seminary, he was ordained in 1897 and served as assistant in the North Reformed Church of Newark, New Jersey. From 1897 to 1907 he was minister of the Congregational Church of Briarcliff Manor, New York. Entering the Presbyterian fellowship, he served for four years as pastor in Morristown, New Jersey.

In Princeton, Harvard, and many other educational institutions, his carefully thought-out sermons, enlivened by his engaging personality, Scotch wit, and deep resonant voice, have made him popular as a university preacher. He wrote in 1909 *A Working Theology*, and in 1923 *The Sheer Folly of Preaching*. He has taken a place of leadership in the activities of his denomination. Rutgers gave him the D. D. degree in 1914.

Doctor MacColl was a church organist in Scotland and before entering the ministry in this country, his last service in this capacity was for the Central Congregational Church in New York City, during the ministry of the Rev. William Lloyd.

Favorite Hymn: "My favorite hymn is Whittier's 'Dear Lord and Father of Mankind,' which seems better, perhaps, than any other to express the spirit in which man makes his approach to God."

IX

THE SOURCES OF SPIRITUAL POWER

Text: Bring me a minstrel. And it came to pass, when the minstrel played, that the hand of the Lord came upon him. —*2 Kings 3. 15.*

THE Bible is a record of divine method as well as of divine truth. It shows us how men lose the sense of God as a vivid reality, and how they may regain it; and it shows this in ways adapted to the mind of the average man. For illustration, I select two incidents in the life of the prophet Elisha.

Three kings—of Judah, Israel, and Edom—have united to punish the king of Moab, a great sheep master who, when King Ahab died, refused to pay further tribute to the king of Israel. The united armies are soon held up by a more destructive foe than Moab. There was no water, we are told, for the hosts, nor for the cattle that followed them—a serious condition. Of course the pessimist was there; he is always there. *"The cause is lost,"* said the king of Israel. *"Alas! that the Lord hath called these three kings together to deliver them into the hand of Moab!"* But, fortunately, the man of resource was also there—

the man who never lies down beneath a difficulty, but finds in it a challenge. *"Is there
not here a prophet of the Lord,"* says the king
of Judah, *"that we may inquire of the Lord by
him?"* How very human, how very much like
ourselves these kings are! Not one of them
had thought of inquiring of the Lord before
they undertook the expedition, but when
trouble and difficulty come, *"Is there not,"*
they ask, *"a prophet of the Lord?"* And there
is. God's word is always near to the man who
sincerely, though tardily, seeks it. It is worth
noting that the kings went down to Elisha;
they did not send for him. This was as it
should be. How small is even a combination
of kings against the man, however weak he
may seem by human standards, who incarnates
the truth of God.

Without a tremor Elisha surveys the kingly
trio. Then his searching gaze fastens itself
upon the king of Israel. The color rises to his
cheeks when he recalls that scene upon the
summit of Mount Carmel, when his great
master, Elijah, stood alone against the prophets of Baal. He hears again the shrieking
voice of Jezebel, and asks, indignantly: *"What
have I to do with thee? get thee to the prophets of thy father, and to the prophets of thy
mother."* But no sooner has he spoken than

his eye rests upon the face of the king of
Judah, and then he knows that he has gone too
far. Once more the one righteous man saves
the day. *"As the Lord of hosts liveth, before
whom I stand,"* he says, *"were it not that I
regard the presence of Jehoshaphat the king
of Judah, I would not look toward thee, nor
see thee."* And then he adds, *"Bring me a
minstrel."* *"And it came to pass, when the
minstrel played, the hand of the Lord came
upon him."*

Why did Elisha send for a minstrel? The
plain truth was that the man of God had lost
his temper badly. The man who on another
occasion cursed the foolish children who
mocked his bald head had again let himself go.
His soul was racked with resentment, hatred,
and contempt. But he knew what you and I so
often forget—that if God was to speak to
him, he must himself be quiet; that if God's
loving purpose was to find utterance through
him, everything in him that had not yielded
itself to the divine will must be put away.
And so he sent for the minstrel.

This is one of several instances in Scripture
in which music furnishes the atmosphere
which makes divine power effective. Saul
meets a company of the prophets coming with
psaltery and timbrel and pipe and harp, and

the Spirit of the Lord comes mightily upon
him and he is turned into another man. Later
the Spirit of the Lord departs from Saul, and
an evil spirit troubles him. At the suggestion
of his servants, he sends for a cunning player
upon the harp, and it came to pass when the
evil spirit was upon Saul, David took a harp
and played with his hand, and Saul was re-
freshed, and was well, and the evil spirit de-
parted from him. Is not this the reason that
the power and the peace of God are often so
unreal to us—that we are so aggressive in pur-
suit of our own judgments and methods that
we have not paused to ask God's will; we are
so racked and restless with worry and fear,
resentment and ambition, that the Divine
Spirit can find no lodgment in us? The guests
in our homes must be congenial; so must the
guests in the inner chamber of the soul. *"He
that dwelleth in love dwelleth in God."*

I notice that in the preparation of his soul
for its great event—the entrance of God—
Elisha uses means. No doubt he prayed, but
also he sent for the minstrel. Pray God that
your soul may always be open to the sunlight
of his love, that you may become an effective
instrument of his will and of his work. Yes,
but also use the means that he has provided as
aids to the keeping sane and strong of all your

powers. Spend all the time you can in the open air—how many an evil spirit from the devil has been dispelled by a day spent in the country! Send too for the minstrel. Use all the aids that music and art and reading and friendship can bring you to drive out thoughts of cynicism and despair, to banish resentment, doubt, and fear, to quicken all the better energies of the soul, and make you receptive to the voice and touch of the eternal.

The other incident is the beautiful completion of this one. The first suggests a process which is negative and preparatory, the dismissal from the soul of all that keeps God out. The second is positive and constructive—the entering in of the hosts of heaven. Elisha finds a certain minister's widow in dire distress—not a thing in the house but a pot of oil, and a harsh creditor without, waiting to take her two sons as bondsmen. The prophet takes charge of the situation in fine style. *"What,"* he asks, *"is in the house?"*—it is always well to know what you have to work with. He calls for vessels, empty vessels, not a few, to be borrowed from all the neighbors. The vessels brought and filled, all of them, with oil, the woman in her wonder and joy cries: *"More vessels, more!"* But the boy says, *"There are no more."* And then we read, *"And*

the oil stayed." Was it a miracle, or simply
an instance of a good man's genial charity?
Is not the real teaching this, rather, that in
the holy commerce of God and man it is always
man who gives out—never God? The resources of divine love and power and peace
open to the children of God are limitless while
there is one empty vessel brought. We must
bring our empty vessels not a few, all our
dormant capacities and energies and talents,
all that environment and opportunity open to
us, empty, not of serious preparation and self-
development, but of all self-will and bitterness and littleness, and not until they are
filled with the fullness of God will the oil stay.
When we have larger and more spiritual desires we will begin to experience in quite new
measure the power of the God in whose presence we live.

To-day, as in the day of Elisha, music plays
an important part in preparation for a pro-
phetic ministry. "Are you getting your sermon ready?" Mr. Moody once asked of a visit-
ing minister, sitting very early one Sunday
morning on his porch at Northfield.

"No," was the answer; "I am getting myself ready, and that is a much more difficult
business."

Many a minister would bear testimony that,

coming to his pulpit fatigued, perplexed, sometimes despairing, sympathetic music from
choir or congregation has lifted him into a
creative atmosphere, cleared the fog, and
opened for him the windows of heaven. "After
singing like that," I heard a minister say to
his choir not long ago, "the best preaching of
which one is capable is inevitable."

What good music does for the minister it
does also for the congregation.

> "A verse may find him who a sermon flies
> And turn delight into a sacrifice."

Herbert's familiar lines have been confirmed
in the experience of many a worshiper who,
coming from the soil and stain of the world,
has been prepared for worship and made ready
to listen for the voice of God by great music
sympathetically rendered. He has confirmed
in his own experience what Sidney Lanier declared to be the final meaning of music—that
"it creates within man a great, pure, unana-
lyzable yearning after God."

Everything, of course, depends upon the
quality of the music and the spirit of those
who render it. It is well frankly to realize
that the day is past when musical programs
constructed without regard to their religious
value, and rendered by voices unprepared for

spiritual service, will solve the church's problem. Musically, we cannot hope to compete with the Sunday concerts now offered in our large cities, nor with the attraction of famous artists brought into our own homes by the marvel of the radio. But in its own field—the preaching of the gospel in sermon and song to troubled and needy folk—the church is without a rival, and where there is sympathetic preparation for every part of its work there need be no fear that it will ever be superseded.

The preparation of the organist and choir for their share in our common ministry is, of course, quite as important as the preparation of the minister. They should be chosen with the same care. When possible, a brief service of preparation should precede each hour of worship. And the fact should often be emphasized that music rendered with conviction and sympathy will be *better music* than music rendered simply in fulfillment of routine duty or of a financial contract. It is said that Richter was conducting once a rehearsal of the "Messiah." When a young soloist had sung a few bars of "I Know That My Redeemer Liveth," he stopped her.

"Daughter," he said, "do you know?"

She answered, "I think I do."

"Well," he said, "you did not sing it as though you did."

She tried again, and this time put into it the deep feeling and conviction of which she was capable. When the solo was finished, the old man walked over to her and kissed her reverently. "Daughter," he said, "I know that you know."

Two suggestions may be made out of a somewhat long experience: one, that there should not be too much music, unless at special musical services, and even then the musical numbers should not be excessive. Many of us who love the musical service have at times sympathized with that bishop who, after a confirmation service in a certain church, was asked by the musical director, elated by the work of his choir that day, "What did you think of the new Te Deum?" Said the bishop, "It gave me a most vivid sense of eternity." We have sympathized with the well-known clergyman who was told by his organist one Sunday that he was going to try out a new baritone at the service, and that he would sing "It Is Enough."

"When will you have it, Doctor?" asked the organist.

"That is a question," was the reply. "I would not want it after the sermon; it would

never do during the offering, but if you will
put it after one of those long drawn-out prel-
udes or interludes of yours, I think it will be
very appropriate."

The choir director can, of course, hit back—
sermons are at times too long.

My other conviction is that in times like
these, when a good many people are perplexed
and distressed, the greater part of the music
should be cheerful. Do not misunderstand
me; I am not in the least interested in ecclesiastical ragtime or spiritual jazz. But I think
I am not alone in my preference for the major
rather than the minor, for music which sings
to me, "Rejoice in the Lord," or "The Lord Is
My Light," rather than "The Sorrows of Death
Compassed Me," or "I Go Mourning All the
Day." Resolutely retaining the spirit of reverence, we must as resolutely resist the common association of religion with gloom and
the grave. The remark of Oliver Wendell
Holmes is often quoted, that he would probably have been a minister if the minister who
called at his father's house when he was a boy
had not looked and talked so much like an
undertaker. Many a church service fails to
be helpful because the "gladness," which is
one of the dominant notes of the New Testament, is lost in a choral dirge.

STANLEY ARMSTRONG HUNTER, after graduating from Princeton University under the presidency of Woodrow Wilson, taught for two years in Ewing Christian College, Allahabad, India. During his course in Union Theological Seminary he served as assistant in the Central Presbyterian Church of New York City, later acting as temporary pastor of the Church of the Pilgrims at Brooklyn. Called as assistant for the summer of 1914 in the Presbyterian Church, Bryn Mawr, Pennsylvania, he was ordained by Chester Presbytery and remained in charge for a year during the illness of the pastor, the Rev. Andrew Mutch, D. D., returning to Union Seminary for his final year of theology.

After a seven-year pastorate in the North Presbyterian Church, Pittsburgh, Pennsylvania, in January, 1924, he went to Saint John's Presbyterian Church, Berkeley, California, adjacent to the University of California. Occidental College conferred an honorary D. D. degree in 1925. He is an advisory member of the committee on the Revision of the Book of Common Worship of the Presbyterian Church.

Favorite Hymn: "Joyful, Joyful, We Adore Thee," by Dr. Henry van Dyke, "chosen partly because it is from the pen of one of my teachers and because it is a favorite of my congregation."

X

THE FIRST CHRISTIAN HYMN—
MARY'S "MAGNIFICAT"

Text: My soul doth magnify the Lord, and my
spirit hath rejoiced in God my Saviour.—*Luke
1. 46-47.*

ONE of the advantages of a new translation
of the Bible like Dr. James Moffatt's is that
the poetical passages are clearly indicated.
The first part of First Corinthians 13, Saint
Paul's matchless hymn in praise of love,
should be printed as a poem. Embedded in
the narrative of Scripture like precious gems
that sparkle with beauty are some hymns.
Near the beginning of Luke's Gospel is a
Christmas carol. Before the angels sang over
the Bethlehem hills there was a song of joy in
a woman's heart. Saint Luke seems to have
been fond of poetry, and his Gospel has pre-
served three of the ancient hymns of the
church. In the back of most of our hymnals
are to be found the chants: the *Magnificat* of
Mary, the *Benedictus* of Zacharias and the
Nunc Dimittis of the aged Simeon. They are
from the Gospel that has been called "the most

beautiful book in the world." When Mary
visited Elisabeth, her cousin, in the hill country, with a burst of rapturous and wondering
praise in which her full heart runs over, she
gave voice to what we may well call the first
Christian hymn. Women from the beginning
have enriched our faith with their hymns, even
though the church has been tardy in ordaining
them to its highest offices. In some churches
the *Magnificat* is part of the Evensong, but in
the worship of most churches this great hymn
is unfortunately overlooked. The words show
that the social gospel is no new thing:

"My soul magnifies the Lord,
  My spirit has joy in God my Saviour;
  For he has considered the humiliation of his
    servant.
  From this time forth all generations will call
    me blessed,
  For he who is Mighty has done great things for
    me.
  His name is holy.
  His mercy is on generation after generation,
  For those who reverence him.

"He has done a deed of might with his arm,
  He has scattered the proud with their purposes,
  Princes he has dethroned and the poor he has
    uplifted,
  He has satisfied the hungry with good things
  And sent the rich away empty.

He has succoured his servant Israel,
Mindful of his mercy—
As he promised our fathers,
To have mercy on Abraham and his offspring
  forever."   —(*Moffatt's Translation.*)[1]

Although resembling the song of Hannah in
1 Sam. 2. 1-10, which has been called the Old
Testament *Magnificat*, comparison will show
its superiority.

"And Hannah prayed, and said:
 My heart exulteth in the Lord,
 Mine horn is exalted in the Lord:
 My mouth is enlarged over mine enemies:
 Because I rejoice in thy salvation.

"There is none holy as the Lord;
 For there is none beside thee:
 Neither is there any rock like our God.

"Talk no more so exceeding proudly;
 Let not arrogancy come out of your mouth:
 For the Lord is a God of knowledge,
 And by him actions are weighed.

"The bows of the mighty men are broken,
 And they that stumbled are girded with
   strength.
 They that were full have hired out themselves
   for bread;
 And they that were hungry have ceased:
 Yea, the barren hath borne seven;
 And she that hath many children languisheth.

---

[1] Reprinted by permission of Richard E. Smith, Inc., publisher, New York.

"The Lord killeth, and maketh alive;
  He bringeth down to the grave, and bringeth up.

.   .   .   .

  He raiseth up the poor out of the dust,
  He lifteth up the needy from the dunghill,
  To make them sit with princes,
  And inherit the throne of glory:
  For the pillars of the earth are the Lord's,
  And he hath set the world upon them.

"He will keep the feet of his holy ones,
  But the wicked shall be put to silence in dark-
        ness;
  For by strength shall no man prevail.

"They that strive with the Lord shall be broken
        to pieces;
  Against them shall he thunder in heaven:
  The Lord shall judge the ends of the earth;
  And he shall give strength unto his king,
  And exalt the horn of his anointed."

There are better songs than this by far in the
Old Testament, which has its own peculiar
rules of rhythm of sense rather than sound.
The best English translation cannot be expected to bring out the poetry of the Hebrew
original.

The *Magnificat* is of greater significance
than we are apt at first to realize. It should
not be minimized, but magnified. Since its
terminology is derived from Old Testament
sources, it is an interesting link between the

Old and the New Testaments. Has Christian tradition been right in associating it with Mary? There is much sentimentality about our celebration of Mother's Day, when tears are shed over the hymns "that mother used to sing." There was nothing weak or insipid or sentimental about the hymn that tradition associates with the mother of Jesus. It was the music of the trumpet rather than the lute. It should be an antidote to some of our mawkish, sugary songs which profane the sanctuary. It has rightly become her song because it represents her spirit and reflects her personality. The generation that followed did not feel it to be incongruous with her life. In the beginning she offers praise to God with all the powers of her soul, and with her spirit, which means her reason, emotions and will. Next she refers to the distinction given to her in becoming the mother of the Incarnate Son of God. Too many of our hymns are introspective, but this does not remain on a self-centered level. In verses 51 to 53 she rises to larger views of God's purposes in the shaping of human history. His presence and power are vindicated in the humbling of the proud dynasties of the past and in the triumph of the meek. The hymn closes with the expectation that the

assurances given to the fathers of the coming
of the Messianic kingdom will now be fulfilled.
It is thus a great hymn of hope. Where, after
all, do we find better expression of Christian
hope than in the hymnal of the church which
contains such declarations of assurance as
"Jesus shall reign where'er the sun!"

Certainly, the times were not propitious or
hopeful. It matters not how dark may be the
night of despair, there are always those who
hope for deliverance. One commentator in
this connection calls attention to the fact that
birds sing best at dawn before the sunrise.

A study of the phrases of this most striking song in the Bible is bound to bring sur-
prises. Many persons think that religion must
necessarily be a conservative force and that
its value to society consists in inculcating
stability and the acceptance of the *status quo.*
As a matter of fact, this hymn from the mother
of Jesus is revolutionary in the extreme. Ancient literature contains little that is more
radical or revolutionary. Longfellow brought
this out in his poem, "King Robert of Sicily."
The king, hearing the Latin words in the service of the ancient church, asks for their meaning. In indignation over their import he
makes his proud boast. By a sudden turn of
fortune he is reduced to the position of court

jester for years before he comes to his senses again.

Mary sings her hymn of praise to God as the very author of revolutions, as the one who casts down the mighty from their seats and exalts them of low degree. This song looks forward to a complete overthrow of the then existing religious and social order. Power and wealth will be taken from those who selfishly use them, and be given to those who have nothing. Princes will be shaken off their thrones and their crowns given to the humble people of life. This hymn is really a Marseillaise of Reform. Never discount the power of a great song of hope! It left its influence on the early church, which was undoubtedly a singing church. Christianity is known throughout the world to-day as a religion that sings hymns. One of the few references to the early Christians in contemporary literature is to be found in the younger Pliny's letter to Trajan, where he tells how they assembled early before dawn to sing hymns to Christ, their God.

"These that have come hither would turn the world upside down" was the impression of critics of the faith in the book of Acts. But these early Christians were only endeavoring to turn things "right side up." The revolutionary doctrines of primitive Christianity were later glossed over. Do not our hymnals need to-day more sturdy hymns of the social gospel? Every church service ought to include at least one hymn like Frank Mason North's "Where Cross the Crowded Ways of Life," or Louis F. Benson's "The Light of God Is Falling." A few years ago the Survey published one hundred hymns of the social gospel, and some of these have rightly won a place in modern worship. "The Song of the Madonna of the Workshop" was of this order. Probably Jesus received from Mary in the formative years of his youth something of her burning sense of indignation at the world's miseries and wrongs, and from her lips he learned the lesson of championing the cause of the underprivileged and oppressed. What is your favorite hymn which your children will associate with your faith? Does it breathe the sturdy and robust faith of this ancient canticle?

Anyone who protests against the established order of things will probably be considered by our generation a malcontent or a grumbler. Is the church making or breaking prophets to-day? The way of the prophet and reformer has always been hard, as he stands up against social pressure and gives utterance to the words which God whispers to his very soul.

The Bible contains the Magna Charta of human rights. Our hymns are of more influence than our creeds.

Someone has called this first Christian hymn the first rough draft of Christianity. Its dream has never been entirely fulfilled. The very glory of our religion is that its final history has not yet been written. At one time in the early apostolic church efforts were made to fulfill the letter of this song. The hungry were filled with good things even if the rich were not sent empty away. Custom called for a believer to turn over to the apostles his wealth, as we know from Acts 4. 34-35. For a time the early church was communistic, that is, in possession; but not in production. Moreover, the communism was voluntary and not compulsory, which differentiates it from the communism of Russia today. Like every other communistic effort in history, it was a failure. Soon the churches in the outlying districts were asked to take up collections for the poor saints at Jerusalem. Then the church began attacking the problem of the unequal distribution of wealth through charity and almsgiving. Not through charity, but justice will the millennium come, according to the teaching of the prophets.

King Robert of Sicily, holding the selfish ideas that he did, rightly showed indignation when he heard in church this democratic song which visualized the day when Christ would put down princes from their thrones and exalt them of low degree. Wherever Christianity's teachings have been proclaimed this has inevitably happened. The gospel is explosive. Our word "dynamite" comes from the Greek word for power, which occurs again and again in the New Testament. Much of the bitterness against Christianity in many mission lands on the part of those in high places is derived from its inherent democracy. The proud landowner in India who has been accustomed to starve his underlings and beat at will his low-caste menials does not enjoy the spectacle of the return from a mission school or college of a son from an oppressed home ready to accept an administrative position of responsibility in his district. To-day in India low-caste Christian converts give expression in hymn singing to the hope of their hearts, as Negro slaves did in their inimitable spirituals. "He makes the woeful heart to sing." The spread of Christianity has given great impetus to the growth of the democratic idea. We engaged in "the war to end war" with enthusiasm to usher in an era of brotherhood after thrones and crowns had perished. With the emergence of dictatorship in Italy, the curtailment of democracy in many lands and the general debacle of the Peace, the claims of war to be an agent for achieving this end cannot be justified. Christianity, by the spread of its doctrines of the individual's worth and the dignity of common life, is laying foundations throughout the world for the coming structure of democracy.

Mary doubtless had brooded over the fact that "man's inhumanity to man makes countless thousands mourn." She was conscious of the oppression by the Romans of her own people Israel to whom she makes reference. For centuries they had been restive under the foreign yoke. Even in the village of Nazareth there were doubtless examples of the neglect of the poor by those of her own race who were in a position to help. In Jerusalem for thirty-eight years a helpless invalid sat waiting for someone to put him in the way of healing, by the Gate of the Temple called Beautiful! When the time came for her to bring forth her Son, there was no room for them in the Bethlehem inn. Later there may have been real poverty in the Nazareth home. Joseph, the bread-winner, seems to have died early. Jesus, by his reference on more than one occasion to widows, is probably speaking out of a bitter experience of poverty in that humble Nazareth home with its four sons and three daughters. Jesus reserved his highest praise in describing generosity for the widow who cast in her two mites. He seems to have been extraordinarily sensitive to the presence of hunger. It was probably from Mary that he first learned these things. She was not embittered, for she could sing "songs in the night."

There are beauty and inspiration as we know in national hymns. Not all of them are narrow or belligerent. A great nation like ours should give official recognition to "America, the Beautiful," by the late Katharine Lee Bates, because it sounds the Christian note. Some organists at the recurrence of the Armistice season play the national airs to remind the worshipers of the time when we joined with "The Allied and Associated Powers" in dedication to a common cause. National hymns still have power to stir the soul, but the function of the Christian Church is to keep before its worshipers the beauty and inspiration of a universal hymn like the *Magnificat*. It has been well said that just as every nation has its own national hymn, so is the *Magnificat* the hymn of all nations—the hymn of humanity itself.

It is a hymn of joy as well as democracy, joy which does not minimize suffering, but sees that it is not supreme or final. *"My spirit hath rejoiced in God my Saviour,"* is a missing note in modern Christian experience. Some people have just enough religion to make them miserable! They have been baptized in vinegar. Religion to many seems a burden or a duty, but to those of spiritual insight it means sheer joy. The thought of God should set one's spirit aglow with exultant enthusiasm. When Haydn was asked by the poet Carpani why the music which he composed was so cheerful, he replied: "I cannot make it otherwise! I write according to the thoughts I feel. When I think upon God my heart is so full of joy that the notes dance and leap from my pen; and since God has given me a cheerful heart, it will be pardoned me that I serve him with a cheerful spirit." I once listened with delight to a Presbyterian elder, John H. Finley, then president of the College of the City of New York, now editor of the New York Times, as he described the abiding influence upon his own life of his father's favorite hymn. In a humble home of sod, set in the vast prairies of the Middle West, by candle light he would sing, "I'm a pilgrim, I'm a stranger." Wistful it was, but joyful too, for it envisaged a city of permanence and peace—the goal of life.

The cynics of our day sneer at the Puritan and his psalms, but to the stately cadences of "Old Hundred" pioneers have opened roads through the wilderness and laid the foundations of liberty. The note of joy was not missing in their praise.

> "All people that on earth do dwell
> Sing to the Lord with cheerful voice;
> Him serve with fear, his praise forth tell,
> Come ye before him and rejoice."

We Protestants are not unconscious of the debt which the church owes to the mother of Jesus. We think of her faith, her obedience, her humility, and her purity, as well as her tenderness and silent service. But let us not overlook her joy expressed in sacred song. Christian art for a long period delighted in depicting the Madonna and the Child. Art has been well termed the fifth Gospel. The medieval artists introduced the architectural features of their home cities in the background of their paintings, thus bringing Christ to dwell among them. Symbolism abounded; the blue of the Madonna's robe was the sky blue of heaven. But rarely did the artists paint the Madonna singing. One wonders why she is not depicted as using the gift of song which marked the days of maidenhood.

At the approach of Christmas whole cities now join in the ancient carols, medieval music at its best, singing the praise of the Infant Christ in her arms—the Child that was to be called Great. It means much to realize that the mother of our religion's Founder was one whose life ever abounded with praise to God. That is the result of faith. Her spirit envisaged the coming conquest of righteousness over wrong. That is hope. Her heart overflowed with sympathy for the needy. That is love.

O Christian parent, are you by the songs of your home making much of God? That is what the Latin word *Magnificat* means. Is yours a religion of joy that bids you sing, "My soul doth magnify the Lord, my spirit hath rejoiced in God my Saviour"? "We cannot praise God by proxy." It is not enough to sit back in church and let others express the joy of religion. *"Let everything that hath breath praise the Lord."* Beautiful as the offering of music may be, as the poet Gray in his "Elegy" declares, in the sanctuary

"Where through the long-drawn aisle and fretted vault
The pealing anthem swells the note of praise,"

it is incomplete unless every worshiper also brings his own contribution. It is certainly not enough to be a passive listener in the radio congregation. Is yours a home where the songs of Zion are household treasures? Are you teaching them to your children? "You cannot sing what you don't know. Memory must be grooved like the record on the gramophone," says Robert Freeman, in urging parents to store away in the records of their children's memory the songs of the faith to be of help in the night of sorrow or temptation.

> "Come we that love the Lord,
>   And let our joys be known;
> Join in a song with sweet accord,
>   And thus surround the throne.

> "Let those refuse to sing
>   That never knew our God;
> But children of the heavenly King
>   May speak their joys abroad."

OSWALD W. S. McCALL, coming from Australia seven years ago a complete stranger, preached a few days after landing in San Francisco in the First Congregational Church of Berkeley, California, the seat of the University of California, with such acceptance that he was invited to remain in this important field of service. His eloquence immediately attracted attention and the church has steadily grown in influence. A beautiful new colonial edifice has been erected and the radio station KRE has been purchased by the church and the Pacific School of Religion.

He received his education in Melbourne, Australia. During the Great War he was a chaplain with the Australian troops in Egypt and France. This sermon bears witness to his war experiences, which have helped to make him a prophet of international peace on the Pacific Coast.

He was the summer preacher for part of the vacation season of 1929 in the City Temple, London, the pulpit of which he previously supplied in 1924.

He has published two volumes, the first of which, *Cardinals of Faith,* shows the constructive power of his thought. His last book, *The Stringing of the Bow,* reveals marked ability and power in the handling of themes in which young people are interested. He is an artist in words and a preacher of rare power. In every service which he conducts the true atmosphere of worship is created.

Favorite Hymn: "O Love That Wilt Not Let Me Go."

XI

WHEN JESUS SANG

Text: And when they had sung an hymn.—
Mark 14. 26.

I

How is it that Christian art has so missed
this picture of Jesus singing? Surely, if a
cross has become the symbol of the extent to
which his love would go, nothing better than
music could suitably represent that uncon-
querable and wingèd inner life and harmony,
that soaring faith and spiritual experience,
which was his most essential characteristic.
Nothing was more fundamental to him than
this. The song suggests something in him
that is not secondary, no, not even to that
which the cross suggests.

Was his a tenor voice or a baritone? Was
he gifted in song? As he joined with that
group in the second half of the Passover
Hallel, did his voice remain individual among
the others, revealing, as voices have a way of
doing, the man? Listening to those twelve
voices mingling about the table, could one
have detected his as being different, with rich

refinements testifying unmistakably to the
superior personal qualities which made him
greater than his companions?

These are questions bound to arise the moment our fancy begins to play about this
scene, and yet of far more consequence is this,
that he could sing at all at that particular
moment. The lark, pouring forth its song in
the morning sky, a melodious speck lost in the
marvel of the sun, is a lovely and moving fact.
Yet why should it not sing? The sky is open,
the wind is free, the sun is calling! But the
nightingale—what is its secret? Is it from
the black heart of the encompassing night that
it draws its passionate song? Or does it sing
in spite of, even in defiance of, the night?
Whence does it learn that thrilling lay which
mounts as from gloomy caverns and outsings
even the lark's? By this it has captured the
imagination and moved the heart of man more
than perhaps any other bird has done, and
Matthew Arnold is only one of a host whose
spirit has answered to it:

> "Hark! ah, the nightingale!
>   The tawny-throated!
> Hark! from that moonlit cedar what a burst!
>   What triumph! hark—what pain!"

"What triumph! hark—what pain!"—it is

simple to return from this to Jesus! Jesus
has just concluded his solemn introduction to
the disciples of those grim symbols of suffering and sacrifice, the bread and the wine!—
*"this is my body which is broken, . . . this
is my blood which is shed."* Now in another
moment it will be necessary to correct the
exuberant confidence of Peter, who is about to
vow that he will never, never forsake him.
Alas, he has walked with them, sought to
share his mind with them, prayed with them,
yet, in awful loneliness, he sees they have not
known him. He realizes—pathetic knowledge!
—that even his own and closest are untrust-
worthy still! He is aching to get away, away.
Gethsemane, the garden—perhaps he will
shortly be able to escape for a few moments
there. In the multitude of his thoughts the
throbbing pulses of his overcharged soul are
becoming intolerable. . . . The group is
rising to sing the Hallel. How is it that he
can sing at all? How is it the attempt does
not choke him with its sheer incongruity and
the irony of it?

*"They that carried us away captive required
of us—a song!"* the Master's ancestors, exiled
in Babylon, had complained bitterly long before. *"They that wasted us required of us
mirth, saying, Sing us one of the songs of*

Zion. How shall we sing the Lord's song in a strange land?" There are many who are better able to understand that sentiment than they are the nightingale song of Jesus. Life has been hard with you. You have been thwarted at every turn, beset on this side and that, mocked and sported with by fate. The dreams that filled your youthful years, dreams of what life could be, are pale and withdrawn things to-day. Love and life and people have been disappointing. Even the wreathed laurels you have won from the world are turned indifferently in languid fingers, because those prizes have brought no joy. Life's imperious hungers, are they given, then, only that they may be mockingly starved? In moments of worship you smile sadly at the prayer, perhaps sigh a little wistfully; at every note of praise or gratitude something in you protests bitterly; hymns sound in your hearing as clanging cymbals. The lark you can appreciate—we can all sing in the sun; and yet, no, not all of us can do even that! But still fewer of us know the secret of the nightingale. It is far from simple to understand Peter and the others astonishing their jailers with songs in prison. Gray stone walls and prison bars are not the place for song! . . . How is it the Hallel did not stick in the

throat of the Great Master, choking his effort
to sing?

II

Did the explanation lie in a sanguine temperament?   Was he so natively cheerful,
sunny, hopeful, that troubles lay light upon
him and fell from him with ease?   In psy-
chology the opposite of the sanguine temperament is the melancholic—which, of course,
must be no more interpreted to mean melancholy than hysteria should be understood to
signify hysterics.   To a physician the word
"hysteria" is technically used to designate a
certain state of nerves, and as one may suffer
from hysteria and yet never have hysterics,
so may one have the melancholic temperament
without being the victim of melancholia.   The
melancholic temperament is quick to feel the
tragic side of life.   Troubles weigh heavily.
The shadow of things is felt.   There are other
people, however, who are constitutionally in-
capable of seeing or feeling this profoundly.
If circumstances for a moment insist that they
shall, they may make a great outcry, but soon
emerge again blithely into the light, the light
of their own cheerful dispositions.   Inasmuch
as tragedy is as truly a part of life as pleasant-
ness, that temperament is not wholly sound

which is unable to realize it. To be overinflated in rosy good cheer is as ill balanced as to be overdepressed in doleful morbidity. Like all really great men, Jesus was a fine blending of both temperaments. If the sanguine was the stronger in him, this does not mean that he was in any sense akin to either Micawber or Pollyanna. On the contrary, if you are curious to know what filled his mind at this moment, your curiosity may speedily be satisfied. There, standing with the others, preparing to sing, he is even already gloomed and tormented with those cruel spiritual problems and emotions which in a few minutes will be uttering themselves so passionately in Gethsemane, startling the night with a testimony to inward distress so deep that all listening ages since have shuddered in sympathy!

III

Very well. Then the sanguine and the melancholic, the expansive and the contractive types were both in Jesus. The significant question for us now is, How did he win that ascendancy of the expansive, that "life abundant," which he not only urged upon others, but made characteristic of himself? For—he is *singing!* The contractive man—or mood— does not sing! The hurt shellfish draws into its shell. It is a time of hurting for Jesus, yet he is not in his shell. He is singing. How do you account for that?

Was it because he happened to be at the moment in an expansive mood that he was able to sing? Or was it, on the contrary, his singing that made him expansive? Did the mood cause the song or did the song cause the mood?

In an expansive mood in an hour like that? I should, rather, say that if he be not tempted now to contraction, it is because he is not human. But he is human, every line of him. In the circumstances of that severe hour a sensitive soul such as his could not but quiver painfully and experience an impulse to draw within himself. I can suppose there was a moment when effort was required ere he could yield himself to the Hallel, an effort of will not unlike that tugging at the oars whereby a boat is impelled away from the bank and out into the stream. Once in the stream the current captures it and it moves onward. The broad stream of the song could carry Jesus upon it to expansion and depth again, but first he must get there. Yes, he must have been tempted to contraction. But inasmuch as he *sang*—which the contractive does not do—we have a right to assume that he somehow made the transition to expansion, recovering again his own abundant life.

And here, surely, is one of the great ministries of music, and not least of church music.

If church choirs throughout the land could realize more that unto them is intrusted the wizard key with which they may unlock chains and bars from the cramped souls of men, I think singers would consider no study in deportment too slight, no fitness in behavior so trivial, but they would wish to cultivate it, lest by carelessness they should weaken anywhere this ministry. Singing for the emancipation of men, their music would grow richer and more moving, yet as music only can when touched by human sympathies and spiritual insight.

Moreover, if we preachers were more possessed of the liberating contribution that hymns can make to life, I think we would select them with more care. I think we would not despise a moment's effort to appreciate the tangle and the torment quivering in the lives of many of the sentient souls who will be gathering to worship; more human and prayerful thought might accompany our search for appropriate hymns. We would remember that not all the sermons ever preached would be adequate to the condition of some people before us, but that some dear melody of heaven, spreading its soft wings toward the upper air, might succeed, as an eagle carrying its young, in lifting them again to where the blessed are.

And if the people who gather in our church pews throughout the land could but understand better the healing and the liberating, the inspiring and the comforting virtues lying in the sacred music they hear, there would be less absence of mind in the presence of it, there would be more surrendering of oneself to it, more arousing of oneself to attention, more effort to launch upon that harmonious stream which flows toward abundant life.

IV

For the great thing that music does is the liberation of the emotions, without which a man is all tied and knotted within. What virtue to me to know what is right if my heart be not warmed to do it? What care I how fair things be if they be not fair to me, my heart being poisoned against them? From my crabbed heart even your grandest truths will provoke only a snarl unless you can find a way to set me free from myself.

Great emotion universalizes one. It does it with one's past, for example. What memories, faces, voices float out from the hinterland as the heart is moved by music! This crazy little moment that houses our complaint is suddenly expanded into all the years that we have lived, years that have known laughter and love, bright eyes and tender speeches, and the divine hopefulness of youth. Such is the influence of music.

Furthermore, emotion sets us free to mount and mingle again with our best, that highest which is in us all. We look into its face, we realize its kingly beauty and we recognize it as our own. From the swine trough we stand up and with a sob think of the Father's house, and our feet begin to falter homeward. All things good and beautiful and true that have ever touched our life suddenly are longed for and believed in. The hyena of cynicism slinks off into the dark, taking with it its destroying laugh, as waves of a new day wash the east and flood the world with happy light and warmth. In the glory of the great emotion we become one with all truth.

And one with all humanity too. The selfish man's ingrowing death, from which he suffers and chokes, pitying himself, hugging himself, and sinking ever further into shadows, suddenly yields to the broad pulse that had seemed dead in him. He is a man again. The

in-turned heart looks out. His sympathies
and hopes are mingled with humanity. He is
saved by a grand expansion. Thus does he
come to himself.

And, be it observed, the emotion that did it
was not kindled by a fiction. Music is truth.
Music, as one tells us, "comes speaking the
highest wisdom in a language our reason does
not understand because it is older and closer
and deeper than reason." But this ageless
truth told in music, in a hymn for instance, is
not, primarily, perhaps not at all, in the
words. When a group of men are singing rol-
licking club or college songs, is it the words
they are enjoying? Nothing could be more
irrelevant, even more inane than some of the
words they sing, and yet are they critical of
them? They are intelligent men, but on they
go with their roaring, ridiculous song. It is
because there is something in it that is larger
than words, something in the music, the very
spirit of jollity; and even the words, which
could never sustain intellectual scrutiny,
actually by their very absurdity seem to contribute something to that spirit.

How strange, then, that the moment some
men enter a church, they feel that they must
treat music differently! Because the words
of some hymns do not wholly accord with reli-

gious opinions they may hold, or because an Oriental figure of speech employed is not altogether palatable to their Occidental tastes, they refuse to abandon themselves to the truth the hymn is trying to teach. We are not given powers of discrimination to use thus to our hurt, and it is no mark of intelligence when we do.

Had Jesus been guilty of this sort of shallow intellectual captiousness, he could never have sung the Hallel. Some of the sentiment he would have found quite appropriate: *"The sorrows of death compassed me, and the pains of hell gat hold upon me: I found trouble and sorrow. Then called I upon the name of the Lord; O Lord, I beseech thee, deliver my soul. Gracious is the Lord, and righteous; yea, our God is merciful. . . . Return unto thy rest, O my soul; for the Lord hath dealt bountifully with thee. For thou hast delivered my soul from death, mine eyes from tears, and my feet from falling."* Our Master would have had no difficulty with those words. Nor with these: *"The Lord is on my side; I will not fear: what can man do unto me?"* But how do you think he could manage these: *"All nations compassed me about: but in the name of the Lord will I destroy them. They compassed me about; yea, they compassed me about: in the*

*name of the Lord I will destroy them. They
compassed me about like bees; they are
quenched as the fire of thorns: for in the name
of the Lord I will destroy them."* There is
something in this that is very alien to the
spirit of Jesus. Yet there is also something
gloomily terrible and suitably fitting to the
circumstances blackly conspiring around him
now. The great earnestness of the Master's
mind would forbid intellectual trifling, and
amid the chaff of things that were not for him
he would sift out the wheat in the great Hallel
and feed his soul upon it. This he could do
the better because the real truth in music does
not lie in what the words say. Happy when
the words are greatly contributive, but to the
really earnest soul it would be hard indeed to
find in any hymn words so unsuitable as entirely to prevent the truth that is greater than
words.

For the truth lies primarily not in the
words, but in the music, and not only in the
music of notes and harmonies, but also in the
music of the poetry, in the rhythm of the
words. Long ago when minstrels roused or
subdued courts with their minstrelsy their
singing was often nothing more than a chant.
The rolling rhythm of a poem—some Chan-
son de Roland—independent of cleverly con-

structed melodies, and solely by virtue of what was in itself, could march and beat and throb until it awakened the pulses of men and carried men's blood with it. The same ideas cast in prose would have had no such effect.

V

Truth is in music, then, wherever music is found! Alas, if the music listened to should represent only such truth as is liberating to the savage or the beast in one! There is unfortunately too much of that type about. What a damning exposure a man makes of himself when, though able to revel through long hours with some of the popular music that knows so well how to set free the baser passions in man, he yet stands bored and absent in church while the great hymns of the centuries are being sung! What type of truth has that man been accustoming his soul to? and what ears of his soul has he been stopping up, what eyes of his soul has he been darkening, what fine apprehensions dulling that he stands thus dead to the anthems of the gods? In the "Ride of the Valkyries," those wild women of Scandinavian myth whose business it was to charge into battle and name the warriors appointed to die, we are made to listen to their galloping thunder through the clouds, to many wild cries and noises, until primitive hate, wrath, terror, and gloomy power rise up in the terrible music to utter themselves within us as they have been felt by men from the beginning. The "Dead March From Saul" moves onward in solemnly measured beat, drumming awfully the universal truth of bereavement. As one has said, it is not a sorrow we listen to, but sorrow, sorrow, the great world sorrow, nevertheless "the sorrow that is sublimely one with the universe, that lifts its heart, that holds back its tears, that remembers the beauty and the sacredness of the beloved who has passed away." The "Hallelujah Chorus"—God, Sovereignty, Exultance, they are all there. Great are the words—*"For the Lord God Omnipotent reigneth"*—but the straining exuberance of triumph in the music, the thrilling height of that utterance which seeks to tell the forever unutterable, makes it greater, revealing truths the heart of man has always felt, but which have always been beyond the conceiving of his mind.

VI

The music in which Jesus joined, however, was not of this class. Ancient, solemn, august though the Hallel was, it was just as much and as little one of the great musical compositions of the race as any one of our church hymns is. Yet there is no great hymn you can name that was not originally "writ in the climate of heaven, in the language spoken by angels." It came out from the saintly upper reaches of a soul in touch with God and its words were turned into beauty by the gifted tongue of a poet. Whatever the theology of a hymn, its climate is that of diviner worlds than this, and it is cast in the elevated language of the immortals. This is the climate you breathe as you sing it, this is the speech that graces your tongue. We have, we confess, known other climates, climates that destroy, and other speech, but what refinements await us in the pure deeps of a noble hymn!

Some time ago I heard a number of children bawling and yelling facetiously George Matheson's "O Love That Wilt Not Let Me Go." My mind harked back to a scene in France where three men in khaki stood beside the still form of another at their feet. They were getting ready to bury him. For years he had gone through the horror, his loved ones ten thousand miles away; he had "played the game," "done his bit," had simply ached with homesickness, but had resolutely kept his face to the great task to the end. One of the men standing was a chaplain. The three heads were bowed as he read,

> "O Love that wilt not let me go,
> I rest my weary soul in thee,"

every line lighting up, every great truth of the great hymn burning its message in the heart, glorifying the mud and the agony, revealing meaning in the meaningless, life in the arms of death. "O Cross that liftest up my head," he read, his solemn voice somehow seeming to shed sublimity upon that still form lying on that torn, grim earth. "I lay in dust life's glory dead"—and then the effulgent and triumphant close—

> "And from the ground there blossoms red,
> Life that shall endless be."

That hymn was born in the moment of a man's agony and faith, and it needed both to unlock it. How could children have the key? But these men had it, and they will never forget what they saw in it then.

That is one of the secrets of hymns. The lower moods of the soul are not adequate to them. Yet one can rouse himself from lethargy and yield himself to them until he is carried by the song up and out and into the deathless truth that gave it birth. These

sacred songs often find us in much crabbed
and unlovable frame of soul, but they leave us
exalted, liberated, beautified by communion
with that heavenly Thing they enshrine, the
Thing which came into them out of the souls
of fellow men who wrote and sang in their
rarest and holiest hours. Our mood may be
contractive at first, but the song can induce
the wider mood. The effort required to cast
oneself upon the stream can be surprisingly
rewarded. God has ordained this a means of
grace. He has appointed it one of the ways to
new and victorious life.

I shall not press further the futile inquiry
whether Jesus sang because he was in an expansive mood, or whether he induced the expansive mood by singing. The great thing is
that he is singing, and in the shadow of the
cross, *singing*. And the inspiration that is
thrilling through him as he sings is nearer the
ultimate truth than ever was told by philosopher, prophet, or seer.

He who achieves oneness with that truth
goes with singing heart, yes, even through the
valley of the shadow of death, and fears no
evil.

ALBERT WENTWORTH PALMER went to the First Congregational Church of Oak Park, Illinois, in 1924, after serving the Central Union Church of Honolulu for seven years, where was built the imposing Gothic edifice designed by Cram, "The Church in the Garden," the delight of tourists as well as residents of "The Paradise of the Pacific." In 1929 he accepted the presidency of the Chicago Theological Seminary.

Born in Kansas City and graduated from the University of California, he went east to Yale for his theological training, graduating in 1904.

His pastorates in Redlands and Oakland, California, were markedly successful. During most of the ten years in Plymouth Church in Oakland, he taught in the Pacific School of Religion, which conferred on him the D.D. degree in 1922. He served with the army Y. M. C. A. in Siberia.

He has taken an active part in the Rotary Club and many public-spirited enterprises, but has found time to write such books as *The Drift Toward Religion*, *The Human Side of Hawaii*, and *The New Christian Epic*.

Favorite Hymn: "O Master, Let Me Walk With Thee."

XII

THE SINGING HEART

Text: Singing and making melody with your heart unto the Lord.—*Eph. 5. 19.*

CLINTON SCOLLARD writes:

"I met a traveler on the dusty road
  Who bravely bore a heavy load:
  'Stranger, how fare you 'mid life's toil and
      smart?'
  'Comrade,' he said, 'I bear a singing heart!' "

What a wonderful thing to have—a singing heart! Birds have it—listen to them in the morning in the woods in June! Dogs have singing hearts—no one can doubt it who has shared the joy of a dog's companionship on a mountain climb. And flowers and trees? Surely! And lakes and little rivers—beyond a doubt!

But how about people? We've all known some at least who made melody unto the Lord with their inmost souls.

Phillips Brooks was such a one. A Boston paper once contained this line: "The day was dark and gloomy, but Phillips Brooks walked down through Newspaper Row and all was bright." People crowded Trinity Church not merely because an orator spoke from its pulpit, but because the sunshine of a radiant Christian faith was there, something which gave them encouragement to go on and try again and do better.

Robert Louis Stevenson was such a pilgrim of the singing heart. In spite of illness and exile he could write:

"If I have faltered more or less
In my great task of happiness;
If I have moved among my race
And shown no glorious morning face;
If beams from happy human eyes
Have moved me not; if morning skies,
Books, and my food and summer rain
Knocked on my sullen heart in vain—
Lord, thy most pointed pleasure take
And stab my spirit broad awake;
O, Lord, if, too obdurate I,
Choose thou, before that spirit die,
A piercing pain, a killing sin,
And to my dead heart run them in."

Nor was this merely the exuberance of youth with Stevenson, for note those Vailima prayers written in far-away Samoa just before he died: "Give us to go blithely about the business of the day," "Let cheerfulness abound with industry," "When the day returns, call us with glad morning faces, eager to labor, eager to be happy, if happiness shall be our portion, or, if the day be marked for sorrow, strong to endure it."

Richard Lovelace, singing out of hard experience, "Stone walls do not a prison make," and Saint Francis of Assisi, God's troubadour, chanting his canticle of the Sun along the Italian hillsides, are other members of this age-long fellowship of pilgrims of the singing heart.

Not all good people belong to this special company, however. Raphael had a singing heart, but not Michael Angelo—his soul was too deeply bowed before the tragedy of his age. Shakespeare had it, but not Dante, wandering through the realms of gloom, the voice of seven silent centuries. Longfellow had it, but not Lincoln, bearing the burden of his divided country. There seem to be great tragic souls in history who suffer vicariously for their day and generation, whose hearts might have sung most gloriously had not the sin and darkness of the age prevented.

The question inevitably arises in this connection: Did Jesus have a singing heart? Surely he did! Think of his joyous appreciation of birds and flowers and children. Listen to the Sermon on the Mount with its succession of "blesseds." Even in the upper room he says, *"Peace I leave with you, my joy I give unto you."* Can't you hear them singing together around the table before they went out to the Garden of Gethsemane? Singing just before Gethsemane—think of it! I wonder what they sang? A psalm, undoubtedly, but which one? The twenty-third? Or the one hundred and third—*"Bless the Lord, O my soul"?* Or was it the thirty-seventh—*"Fret not thyself because of evildoers, neither be thou envious against the workers of iniquity"?* The psalms comprising the Hallel are usually regarded as those sung at the Last Supper. Was it a singing heart that broke on Calvary?

How may we have a singing heart? Maybe there isn't much anyone can do! Possibly it's just a gift—a matter of temperament and disposition, of digestion and chromosomes— either you have it or you haven't, and that's all! Yet possibly something can be done about it, if one begins in time. Anyway, here are some homely, practical suggestions:

First of all, have the right kind of childhood. Normal children have singing hearts. They improvise grand-opera settings for the events of daily life. Do you remember the children singing in the Temple and how Jesus said that if these should hold their peace, the very stones would cry out? Have a childhood, then, which is in friendly contact with nature, a childhood filled with happy play and opportunities for the free expression of a constructive imagination, have friendly, understanding parents and plenty of brothers and sisters and playmates. But chiefly have God's out-of-doors—an ocean or two and some mountains and hills and a little stream and some friendly trees. Singing hearts flourish in such a childhood.

It is also important to have the right kind of a youth. Those early days of independence when the soul finds itself may hush the song or lift it afresh for all the rest of life. If you would have a singing heart, keep honor high, respect and honor womanhood, keep clear of alcohol, master some craft, learn something, keep sweet and remember that youth need not be cynical and sour—these are the pathetic weaknesses of age, to be forgiven in the weak and disappointed, but never in the spring tide of youthful power.

I would also say, discipline yourself if you would have a singing heart. The most beautiful music is often the most difficult, and it is no accident that some of the world's greatest poems have been written in the most exacting verse forms. To shun self-pity is the essence of self-discipline, and he who is never sorry for himself will find his heart singing within him all day long. Go out and sing with your lips when your heart seems dull and breaking and it will join in the chorus.

A fourth prescription for achieving the singing heart is to lose yourself in some unselfish service. No selfish person ever really had a singing heart. How does a physician keep so cheerful in the midst of pain and suffering? Going from one sick bed to another, he might be expected to acquire an increasing load of gloom. But no, he is always thinking of the service he can render, and the helpful ministry of his life fills his soul with cheer. Do not be sorry for missionaries even though facing hardships in foreign lands. Practically all of them are unusually happy people. They are so absorbed in the constant opportunity to do good that life is continually interesting and, consequently, filled with joy. The most unhappy people I know have no real task to which to give themselves. Self-absorbed and self-centered, they are most miserable. If they could only be induced to adopt a child, or start a club in a social settlement, or promote a Scout troop or a Sunday-school class, or do anything sacrificial and whole-heartedly altruistic, their gloom would flee away. No man will die "with all his music in him" if he consecrates himself to some constructive task for others. The music will come out and sing itself into his task.

It is a popular illusion that great success, prosperity and the world's acclaim produce a singing heart. Such is not the case. Indeed, it is more often quite the other way. Joy comes from a spirit of humility. Thiers, the great leader who served France in her deepest need and national discouragement, once said: "Men of principle need not succeed. Success is necessary only to schemers"; and Carl Hilty, a Swiss philosopher, says, in the same vein, "Success is necessary only to cowards!" Wasn't it Saint Paul who put it this way—*"When I am weak, then am I strong"*? Even the "mute inglorious Miltons" who missed the world's acclaim knew the inner joy, although they never had an opportunity to utter it to all the world.

The greatest thing of all to be said about the singing heart is that it is in tune with God. Note the last words of the text: *"singing and making melody . . . to the Lord!"* The faith of the singing heart is this, that at the heart of this wonderful universe, with its boundless energy and mighty law, its beauty, love, and aspiration, there is a Supreme Intelligence—a heart of love, a great Over-soul, whom we call God! Do you remember in Tennyson's poem how Gareth and Linette meeting Merlin ask him the way to Camelot and the meaning of the mysterious music which they hear? And Merlin answers:

> "An ye heard a music, like enow
> They are building still, seeing the city is built
> To music, and therefore never built at all,
> And therefore built forever."

So our Christian faith believes the universe is built to the music of underlying truth and great ideals. There are dark problems, but they are due, we trust, to our limited understanding and to our partial view of something which is yet in process rather than to any fault in the heart of things. But when a man finds God and is found of him, then a deeper music sings itself into his inmost being and his heart chants with the saints of long ago: *"The eternal God is thy refuge, and underneath are the everlasting arms."*

"In the world ye shall have tribulation: but be of good cheer; I have overcome the world."

"Light is sown for the righteous, and gladness for the upright in heart."

"Commit thy way unto the Lord; and he shall bring it to pass."

"*To them that love God all things work together for good.*"

"*I have fought the good fight, I have finished the course, I have kept the faith: henceforth there is laid up for me the crown of righteousness which the Lord, the just judge, shall give to me at that day; and not to me only, but also to all them that have loved his appearing.*"

HUGH THOMSON KERR is known to hundreds of thousands on the Atlantic seaboard as the preacher whose vesper sermons in Shadyside Presbyterian Church, Pittsburgh, are broadcast by KDKA. He was born in Ontario in 1872, and received his B. A. from the University of Toronto in 1894, and his M. A. the following year. While a student at Knox College, Toronto, he was drawn to Western Theological Seminary in Pittsburgh, Pennsylvania, to complete his theological studies. After graduating there in 1897 he remained in Pittsburgh for four years as pastor of the Oakland Church. After pastorates in the First Presbyterian Church, of Hutchinson, Kansas, and Fullerton Avenue Presbyterian Church of Chicago, Illinois, he returned to Pittsburgh in 1913 at the call of the influential Shadyside Presbyterian Church. As a result of his Y. M. C. A. experiences in France during the Great War, he wrote *From Port to Listening Post*.

Doctor Kerr holds the important position of president of the Board of Christian Education of the Presbyterian denomination. He has been a careful and persistent writer, and among his best-known volumes are four series of children's sermons. Worshipers in Shadyside Presbyterian Church would miss his weekly talk to the children.

The college of Emporia, Kansas, conferred upon him the degree of Doctor of Divinity in 1908, as did the University of Pittsburgh in 1918, and Washington and Jefferson College in 1920.

Doctor Kerr collaborated in a missionary volume with Dr. Robert E. Speer after their visit to China and Japan in 1926. His book *The Gos-*

pel in Modern Poetry is a collection of sermons broadcast over KDKA. The Presbyterian Banner each week prints his vesper sermon of the preceding Sunday.

He was elected Moderator of the Presbyterian General Assembly in May, 1930.

Favorite Hymn: "Fairest Lord Jesus."—"The hymn makes an appeal to me because it contains the central thought of the gospel, and its music has a lilt and an uplift which I believe ought to accompany the Christian gospel."

"GOD OF OUR LIFE, THROUGH ALL THE CIRCLING YEARS"

By Hugh Thomson Kerr.

Tune, *Sandon*

God of our life, through all the circling years,
    We trust in thee;
In all the past, through all our hopes and fears,
    Thy hand we see.
With each new day, when morning lifts the veil,
We own thy mercies, Lord, which never fail.

God of the past, our times are in thy hand;
    With us abide;
Lead us by faith to hope's true Promised Land;
    Be thou our Guide.
With thee to bless, the darkness shines as light,
And faith's fair vision changes into sight.

God of the coming years, through paths unknown
    We follow thee;
When we are strong, Lord, leave us not alone;
    Our Refuge be.
Be thou for us in life our Daily Bread,
Our heart's true home when all our years have
    sped.

XIII

"THE GREATEST SONG IN THE WORLD"

Text: Having harps of God, and they sing the song of Moses the servant of God, and the song of the Lamb, saying, Great and marvelous are thy works, O Lord God, the Almighty; righteous and true are thy ways, thou King of the ages. Who shall not fear, O Lord, and glorify thy name? for thou only art holy; for all the nations shall come and worship before thee; for thy righteous acts have been made manifest.—*Rev. 15. 3-4.*

WHEN Aristotle was asked what he thought of music he replied: "Jupiter does not sing, neither does he play upon the harp." The inference is that music is unbecoming in the deity and therefore is unprofitable to man. The Christian point of view is exactly the reverse. The harps of music belong to God and it is he who sets the hearts of men to singing. In the Bible, history is set to music and is written from God's point of view; and from God's point of view *history* issues in victory. This song is a song of victory. The victors stand beside a sea of glass mingled with fire. They had come forth conquerors over the

193

world. Its suffering and sin, its sorrow and shame had been overcome. They had come up out of the bloody conflict with the powers of evil, uncontaminated, unconquered. They had come out of a very furnace of hell and they had come out with a song on their lips and were now standing upon this sea of glass mingled with fire, the symbol of a fiery furnace, at last quiet and at rest, like a summer sunset at sea. In their hands they held the harps of God and they sang the song of Moses and the Lamb.

I

The title of the song is significant. It is the "Song of Moses and of the Lamb." It is the song of Moses, the servant of God, and the song of Jesus, the Saviour of men. It is an arresting title. It joins together the past and the present. It is the song of Moses, the song which he and the ransomed people of Israel sang when they crossed the Red Sea in triumph, when slavery and paganism lay behind them. You remember the song that they sang on the shores of the silent sea and on the threshold of their emancipation: "Sing unto the Lord, for he hath triumphed gloriously: the horse and his rider hath he thrown into the sea." It is not only the song of Moses, however, it is the song of the Lamb, the Lamb of God that taketh away the sin of the world. He too has triumphed, and from his cross he reigns over the consciences and hearts of humanity.

This new song, sung to the music of the harps of God, sings of the victory of God's people down through all the centuries. The law came by Moses, but grace and truth came by Jesus Christ. This song sings of the Old Testament and the New. It sings of the triumph of the law and the triumph of the grace and truth of the gospel. It sings of reformation and of leadership. It sings of social reform and of the new birth. It sings of the victories of struggle and the conquests of peace. It takes up into itself all the major notes of physical and mental, moral and spiritual redemption and weaves them into a song of triumph.

One of the modern musical masterpieces of the world is Dvorak's "The Symphony of the New World," in which we hear the majestic march of the Largo. When you listen to it, you hear all through familiar notes that haunt you. Where did you hear them? Then you realize that you are listening to a masterpiece that has been woven out of the familiar melodies of the Southland, the old spirituals of

the Negro people, born of the sufferings and
sorrows of the days of slavery, dipped in the
tears of exile and separation and baptized into
the hope of freedom.   The master musician
has taken all these familiar melodies and has
lifted them up into a symphonic masterpiece;
and through it you hear the voices of a redeemed people singing their song of hope, and
giving expression to their faith.

So with this new song of Moses and the
Lamb.   Its music is woven into a majestic
triumph song out of the sufferings and sacri-
fices of all the past.   There is nothing somber
or minor about it.   Its majestic, martial music
is set to the theme of victory.   It is the song
of life over death, of joy over suffering, of
resurrection over Gethsemane and Calvary.

II

This, then, is its title: The Song of Moses
and of the Lamb.   *What is its theme?*   Like
all our best songs, it is short.   It is like the
song the lark sings.   It has one piercing note.
It is one perfect verse of Hebrew poetry.
Every line is taken from somewhere out of the
Old Testament.   It is a compilation of verses
taken from the books of Hebrew history, and
its theme is the glory and the greatness of
God.

The song sings, first of all, of the glory of God. "Great and marvelous are thy works, O Lord God, the Almighty." That is the theme of the song of Moses; that is the theme of the song of the gospel. A great song must have a great theme. You cannot sing a great song about something that is trifling or frivolous. To have great music you must have a great subject. Love is a great theme, and love claims some of our greatest songs. Beauty is a great theme, and many of our best songs sing of beauty. Victory is a great theme, and some of our most stirring songs sing of victory. But the greatest of all themes is glory, the glory of God; and the greatest of all our songs are songs that sing of God, his glory and his greatness. "Holy, Holy, Holy, Lord God Almighty." That is a great song with a great theme. "We Praise Thee, O God, We Acknowledge Thee to Be the Lord"—that is a great song and a great theme. If you are going to have a great song, you must sing about something great. If you are going to have a great song, you must have a great theme. That is why many of our so-called gospel hymns are trivial and unworthy. They leave God out. They deal with things that are merely sentimental. That is why some of our modern social service songs are so very heavy-hearted, so argumentative, and drop earthward. It is difficult to sing about ourselves. It is difficult to sing about society. It is impossible to sing about sin. John Ruskin has said that "before you sing you must, first of all, have the right moral state." There must be a moral motive behind art if it is to be great art. Songs are inspired. Jenny Lind speaks of the day and the hour when she became artistically alive. The singer must be inspired. Beauty can inspire. Love can inspire. Hope can inspire; and all these high inspirations are the breath of God blowing through the soul of man.

Stand with Moses by the sea when victory came to him and to his people. Who struck the blow that brought those slaves out into liberty? Who carried them through in triumph? It was God; they themselves were helpless. That was why they sang: "Who is like unto thee, O Lord, among the gods? who is like thee, glorious in holiness, fearful in praises, doing wonders?" Stand beside the empty sepulcher on Easter morning. Who brought victory out of death and defeat? It was God. The amazing thing about our salvation is that it is God who works in us to will and to do his own good pleasure. He takes the initiative. It is not our arm or our

might, but his arm and the light of his counte-
nance that give us the victory. It is God who
comes down to dwell with men. It is God who
is the great Seeker, and when we pause to
think of the fact that God has come into our
lives and lifted us up and redeemed us, then a
new song thrills in our hearts and we sing:

> "It is God; his love looks mighty,
>   But is mightier than it seems:
> 'Tis our Father; and his fondness
>   Goes far out beyond our dreams."

The song sings not only of glory, but of
righteousness, of the righteousness of God.
God's ways are righteous. God's ways are
true and in the end his righteousness comes
forth into the light. Righteousness has the
last word. Righteousness outlives evil. Sin
and evil disintegrate. Truth and righteousness endure. Whatever else may be the purpose and meaning of the mysterious symbols
in the book of Revelation, the one reiterated
theme is that of victory. Throughout all the
strange imagery of the book there is a return
to the recurring theme: "Alleluia: for the
Lord God omnipotent reigneth." Righteousness cannot be thwarted. Truth cannot be
crushed. God cannot be defeated. His throne
is established forever. This is the message

200 MUSIC AND RELIGION

that we need. There are people who talk as if God were dead. They have forgotten how to say, "Lord, thou hast been our dwelling place in all generations." They recall the words only at funerals. They let slip out of their minds the fact that God is not only almighty, but eternal.

Years ago Froude, the historian, published an essay entitled "The Science of History." It was an answer to those who contended that history is just the working out of the consequences of the law of cause and effect; that everything is determined and that history can be reduced to an exact science. Froude denied that contention. He showed in his essay that there are personal, uninvited, and unrecorded forces in history. For that reason we can never know from the past what may transpire in the future. He claimed that the only thing we can get out of history, the only conclusion we can reach, the only principle we can take away from a study of history is that in the end righteousness wins and sin loses out. That is why this song is a song of victory. Born in an age of persecution, it sings of everlasting triumph and goodness. After the persecutions have spent themselves, after the lions have ceased to roar, after the fires have died down, after the sword has been sheathed, then love reigns immortal and God has the last word.

If we are to have singing Christians and a singing church and a singing world, we must put God into the center of life. What America needs more than development of water-power or a new tariff schedule is a new sense of God. We must win our liberty from what this book calls the beast; and when God turns again our captivity to the multitudinous things that claim our homage, then our mouths will be filled with laughter and our hearts with singing.

BURRIS JENKINS is an institution in Kansas City, Missouri, where he was born October 2, 1869, and where for the last twenty-three years he has been pastor of the Linwood Boulevard Christian Church. When he attended its Sunday school as a boy, it met in a room over a store; it has grown under his pastorate from five hundred to three thousand eight hundred members. He was ordained to the Disciples' ministry in 1891, serving for four years as pastor in Indianapolis, then becoming professor of New Testament literature and later president of the University of Indianapolis. From 1901-1907 he was president of Kentucky University.

Doctor Jenkins not only has influenced public opinion from the pulpit, but the press as well. From 1919-21 he was editor and publisher of the Kansas City Post. The radio has brought his message to countless homes in the Middle West. Besides the Sunday school, seven meetings are conducted each Sunday by his church, two of them being afternoon motion-picture services, and one of them a church service in a slum district downtown. All told an average of eight thousand are in attendance. One of the unique features of the busy schedule of his church has been a psychiatric clinic with the co-operation of medical specialists.

He is the author of several books.

Favorite Hymn: "I Love to Tell the Story."

XIV

WONDER, LOVE, AND PRAISE

Text: Raise a song, and bring hither the
timbrel,
The pleasant harp with the psaltery.
Psa. 81. 2.

DR. JAMES MOFFATT, lecturing in Canada in
the summer of 1928, called attention to two of
our great old hymns which contained the
phrase "Lost in wonder, love, and praise."
The first in date is "Belmont," written in the
seventeenth century by Joseph Addison:

"When all thy mercies, O my God,
My rising soul surveys,
Transported with the view, I'm lost
In wonder, love, and praise."

The other is the last stanza of "Beecher," by
Charles Wesley, a few years later, the closing
words of which are:

"Changed from glory into glory
Till in heaven we take our place,
Till we cast our crowns before thee,
Lost in wonder, love, and praise."

Doctor Moffatt says in his comment—and I
think he is correct—that this little phrase

sums up the whole of religion. It is indeed made up of these elements—wonder, love, and praise—and when one loses himself in these three, you may be sure that religion has found him and he has found religion.

Wonder is by no means a childish state; and although children may be lost in it more than the rest of us, this fact only indicates the truth of the word that if we would enter into the kingdom of heaven, we must become as little children. When we have lost the capacity for wonder, when we have become so accustomed to life and all its experiences, its joys and its sorrows, its interests and appreciations, and have become so fixed that we are no longer stirred to admiration, to awe, to hero-worship, to all those nameless emotions which the beauty of the world, its design, its law, and its order create in the heart of the most unsophisticated, then we are pretty nearly through with life; and the unseen and the divine are far removed from us.

What a place of wonder is this world to a little child! Every one of them is an Alice in Wonderland. And the longer we keep this sense of marvel in the glorious creation all about us, the longer do freshness and zest and tang belong to life. Anyone who has walked out into his yard or a public park, or

even along the asphalted city streets on early
fall nights and has seen the mystic moonlight
sifting down through the trees and glorifying
the most ordinary objects with a sheen like
that of aluminum, and has been insensible to
the wonder of it, must be, to say the least,
self-centered and half blind.   And what shall
I say of the Missouri woods, with forest trees
unequaled, to my partial eyes, on all this con-
tinent, when once they have been touched by
the frost and their greenness turned into red
and gold?   Can you look at them unmoved?
Wordsworth is considered to be the first to
put into English verse this natural wonder
and reverence for the mystery and the loveli-
ness in nature, although that love and reverence must always have been there, even if inarticulate.   It was not true of him alone, but
of millions of others that "My heart leaps up
when I behold a rainbow in the sky!"   The
host of golden daffodils has flashed upon many
another inward eye that is the bliss of solitude.   If you happened to see it recently, you
could not help but be transported by the sight
of the blood-red sun that set over Kansas and
painted the sky vermilion for twenty million
miles up to the top of heaven.   The sense of
law and of beauty, the wonder in which savage man first lost himself, was the dawning

of religion in his half insensate heart. I think
it is something like this that Vachel Lindsay
means when he sings:

> "Go find the wonders of the dawn,
> And bring the wonders down.
> Ring, ring the wonders down,
> Bring, bring the wonders down."

Constantly man himself is striking the rest
of the world with wonder, keeping alive and
fostering, perhaps without intending it, the
elements of religion. The marvels of his
scientific discovery and invention have over-
powered us these last fifty years. You cannot sit before the radio, common as it is, without still marveling at the strangeness and the
uncanny magic of it all. At least I can't. Can
you remember the thrill a few short years
ago when you first saw an airplane sailing like
a silver minnow in the sky? My own heart
beat fast and my throat half choked when I
first saw those young knights of the air circling over the battle lines of France. This
is an everyday sight now; and almost everybody has been up; but our souls are dead if we
do not still wonder. Somebody announced the
other day that he was growing a new vege-
table which was potato below ground and
lettuce or cabbage or something else above

ground. Some college boys are growing blue-
berries in New Jersey an inch in diameter.
What will be done next? It was only a few
years ago that insulin was discovered and the
dread of diabetes was banished. I have myself seen patients snatched from the jaws of
death by means of it. To-morrow it will be
something else—a sure cure for cancer. God
knows what. We all wonder what it will be,
and the wonder is good for us. It is the root
of religion.

There was a Man once who excited wonder
in everybody his life touched, and is still,
after nearly two thousand years, stirring the
awe, the admiration, the hero-worship of the
world. God sent him a-purpose for just that.
His mother, Mary, wondered when she con-
ceived him, and still more when she bore him,
and when shepherds and great philosophers
came into the little stable to kneel by his
manger cradle. She kept all these things and
pondered them in her heart. The old men in
the Temple, when he talked with them at
twelve years of age, wondered at his understanding and his answers. The people of his
village, when they heard him talk in his early
youth, only thirty years old, wondered where
this man got all his wisdom, having never
learned. The crowds that followed him and

listened to his golden voice uttering such things as they had never heard before heard him gladly and wondered at his strength and beauty. Pilate looked into his face, even after he had been condemned to death, and was struck almost speechless with awe and wonder. And all down through the centuries, and through all the lands of the earth, wherever the story of his life and death has been told, men white and black and brown and yellow have echoed with bated breath, "Greater love hath no man than this," and have bent the knee. Surely, it was for this that he was sent —to give birth to wonder, to add to the already overwhelming mystery of the world, by the unfathomable enigma of his beauty, his charm, his strength and self-abnegation.

Everything in the world is full of mystery —birth, death, and all that comes between: friendship, the pull of one personality for another, the power of one mind over another, unspoken communication, the unconscious forces that work in our lives—nine tenths of our being, they tell us, is unconscious—love, the power of music, the beauty of tragedy, war, storm, darkness, and light. We are walking in a fairyland, a mid-summer night's dream; it all seems at times utterly unreal and yet it is so beautifully or so terribly real. The sense of this puzzlement, this unfathomable mystery —that sense is the very beginning of contact with the Unseen, the Almighty, the Eternal. It is the rudiments of religion, and we all possess it.

Then it takes love to help make religion— all kinds of love. The fact that all our hearts have loved is testimony to the universality of our religion. He is most religious who loves best all things both great and small. Does he love life? He is religious. Does he love the woods and the streams, the hills and the plains? Just in so far is he religious. Does he love animals, dogs, cats, birds, butterflies, and take delight in their ways and their manners? Just that much is he religious. If some of these things he does not love, a little slice of his religion has been cut off by some untoward incident in his early childhood.

The profoundly religious person loves people; he cannot help it, no matter how unlovely people may be in certain moods and at certain times. He may get very impatient because so many people are still only twelve years old and cannot see anything in a large and grown-up way; but if his heart is right, he cannot, he simply cannot, cherish any ill will, but only tolerance and a sort of amused regret. We are learning a lot about the inside workings of human minds and hearts, and in the next fifty years we are going to learn a whole lot more. When we do, we shall see as if through plate glass into the motives that cause people to act as they do, that cause their minds to think as they do, and then we shall find it impossible to hate anybody, to fight anybody, to go to war with anybody, to condemn anybody.

That was a great Psychologist who, two thousand years ago, gave one single command, one only, and that was, "Love!" Imperative mood. Second person singular. Directed at every one of us. It was no foolish command. He meant by it for us to let loose all the pent-up emotions of our hearts, the natural instincts to benevolence, to love everything and everybody, all kinds of love. We know how to love our own: our children, we'd die for them; our friends, we'd spend ourselves day or night for them. We know what love is; nobody needs to tell us. We have that much religion in us, all of us. The great Master only meant to turn loose that same floodtide of love which we now pour out so extravagantly for the few and with it inundate the world. Nothing unreasonable about it.

If one has such wonder and such love, he

can no more withhold praise than he can hold his breath. Praise is instinctive to the religious heart, which means all hearts to greater or less degree. As you look upon the beetling crags of a mountain canyon, or the white and silver foam of a cataract, or the russet and golden woods of the autumn, you cannot repress the upward rush of emotion. As you walk down the street on a crisp and golden autumn morning, with shoulders straight and chest thrown out and breath coming rich and deep, you are unconsciously offering praise to that great mind and heart which has given the unspeakable boon of life. Somebody has said that praise is earth's highest art; yes, it is more than that, it is earth's most irrepressible instinct. Half our religious worship is made up of praise, and the other half more than shot through with it.

It is not that we add anything to the Creator's dignity and power by praising him. It is not that we tickle his egoism or satisfy his thirst for adulation. He cares no more for these things, of course, than he did for the blood of lambs and of bullocks. We can add nothing to his glory by telling him how great he is, and how beautiful and how wonderful. It is, rather, that we lift ourselves up by a recognition, vocal or inarticulate, of all the

beauty of his mystery. It is only that we fill
the lungs of our own souls with air, clear and
pure, that freshens our own spiritual blood
streams. Praise is only looking up, after all.
Praise is aspiration. Praise is the tribute we
pay to that which we would like to emulate
and in even the feeblest fashion to grow like.
It is not, then, futile to sing to Him and of
him, to pray to him and, as we say, exalt him.
We can't help it. It is as natural as breathing,
the beating of the heart, the constant reaction
of the nerves. It keeps us alive, makes us
stand up straight, carries us through storms
or through heat. Praise is the consciousness
of the Eternal in our minutest affairs and the
aspiration after him in our profoundest
affairs.

Then the last word is the first word, "I am
lost—lost in wonder, love, and praise." What
a blessing it is to be lost! The trouble is we
are so afraid of being lost, when in reality it is
the greatest good fortune that can befall us.
We never really live until we lose ourselves in
something. What a boon to lose oneself in
one's work, to be drugged with it, to be drunk
with it, to lose all thought of self in it! Never
was truer word than that of Jesus, "Whoever
saves his life shall lose it, and whoever loses
his life shall save it." Now and then—just

now and then—I see somebody completely lost
in his life's work. What a sight that is!
How uplifting, how inspiring! It is the narrow road, and few there be that find it. For
most of us, self is so much alive and so seldom lost. Just now and then we see somebody
absolutely lost in wonder, admiration, hero-
worship—what a thrill it gives us merely to
stand off and see it! Now and then—just
now and then—we see somebody lost in love,
all thought of self gone, forgotten, obliterated,
in devotion to the beloved object or cause.
There is no sight like it on this poor love-
starved earth. Now and then—just now and
then—we see somebody lost in praise, contemplation, meditation, aspiration, with a wrapt
and upward look beyond all the shadows
round about; and then we begin to understand
what it is to lose one's life to gain it. The
world well lost! A happy thing to be lost!
The greatest boon in human life to be absolutely and irretrievably lost—lost in wonder,
love, and praise. If anybody can accomplish
that for us, for you and for me, it is Jesus,
our Master, our blessed Lord.

Dr. George Stewart, the gifted pastor of the Presbyterian Church at Stamford, Connecticut, is the author of several books. He collaborated with Professor Henry B. Wright, of Yale, in two volumes, *The Soldier's Spirit* and *The Practice of Friendship,* and in 1925 wrote the *Life of Henry B. Wright.*

At Yale, after taking his A.B. degree in 1915 and his LL.B. degree in 1917, he served as general secretary of the Y. M. C. A. for two years and was awarded the degree of Doctor of Philosophy. In Madison Avenue Presbyterian Church, New York City, he was an associate of Dr. Henry Sloane Coffin. With Dr. Adolph Keller of Switzerland, he wrote *Protestant Europe, Its Crisis and Outlook.* European church life is well known to him.

He is in close touch with students, as he is in demand as a speaker at student conferences. Student groups as well as churches have found his two devotional books helpful and inspiring.

Favorite Hymn: "Immortal Love, Forever Full."

XV

PRAYER AND MUSIC IN WORSHIP

A SERVICE of worship, and particularly a public prayer, is not an expression of feeling of the leader. He is a representative of the group, an impersonal voice crying out the adoration and thanks and humiliation of those who worship. Through him and through liturgy and hymn embarrassed human creatures lose their identity, escape the inhibitions with which reticence and a sense of privacy bind them down, finding voice through him to make their *credo,* whisper their confession, and pronounce their hope. A subjective type of worship thwarts this process. Doctor Munger put the matter crisply when he said, "We do not worship because we feel like it, but that we may feel."

Prayer and music are the most neglected elements in public worship. He who leads in public prayer will do well to consider what prayer is. He must remember that as a leader of the prayers of others he is not wrestling before the Lord, like Jacob at the brook Jabbok, with his personal difficulties, but is conducting the group into vital contact with God.

The opening prayer will be short and will concern itself largely with praise and the affirmation of some particular attribute of God. The longer prayers, which should never be over three minutes (better if only two), will have ample room to include other elements.

Prayer has many moods and offices. In one of its aspects it is sheer ascription of praise, an expression of adoration. The Old and the New Testament both offer many effective ideas for the opening sentences of public prayer. "O Thou who inhabitest the praises of Israel," "O thou Ancient of Days," "O Thou who leadest thy people like a flock," are suggestive. A public prayer, in its opening, centers the thought of the people on God best when it is adoration of God as an end in himself.

Thanksgiving is another element which should follow rapidly upon adoration. General terms are never as helpful as specific objects for which men and women or boys and girls have reason to be grateful. Deliverances from illness, escape from sharp temptation, persistence of employment, love and affection, and, best of all, the beauty, the charm and the merits of Jesus, are all objects which lie close to human hearts. Thanksgiving expressed in truthful, beautiful concrete terms will be a factor in any longer prayer. The language must be sonorous, dignified, beautiful, never of the market place.

Petition in which the leader in orderly language lays before the throne of grace the necessities and hopes of the worshipers will be a feature of the longer prayer. The leader will do well to avoid redundant verbs and phrases. The constant refrain of "give us" or "we beseech thee" may mar an otherwise effective prayer.

Intercession is yet another element of prayer, better expressed in simple phrases than in long generalizations. If intercession is made for "all sorts and conditions of men," it is well to follow it with a brief list of particular kinds of men. A modified litany form, omitting the customary responses of the people, is effective.

Confession is an important element of any service of worship. It should not occupy a large place in the opening prayer, which should be only a cry of adoration and praise; and when confession is once introduced in some intermediate prayer it should not make another appearance in the service. If it appears in some longer prayer only, it should appear but once in that utterance.

The bidding prayer is effective, wherein the

leader directs the minds of the worshipers to specific objects. The following is an example:

A Bidding Prayer

(*The people seated and bowed, or kneeling.*)

Let us pray that God will give us sensitive hearts that we may be aware of the gift of human friendship.

(*Here followeth a period of silent prayer.*)

Let us give thanks for forgiveness which knows no measure, and for love that remembers no more our iniquity and utterly forgets our sin and error.

(*Here followeth a period of silent prayer.*)

Let us bless God for courage we have received through the heroism of those who have rescued us from danger in peril of themselves.

(*Here followeth a period of silent prayer.*)

Let us pray that by the compassion given unto us we also shall be able to aid others in days of overwhelming need.

(*Here followeth a period of silent prayer.*)

Let us give thanks for the understanding of friends who have loved us when we have been unlovely, and have created within us by their trust new hopes, new courage, and new purpose.

(*Here followeth a period of silent prayer.*)

Let us praise God for the faith of men and women whose steadfastness in adversity has often re-established our own belief.

(*Here followeth a period of silent prayer.*)

Let us give thanks for love which suffereth long and is kind, which hopeth all things, believeth all things, endureth all things, and never faileth.

(*Here followeth a period of silent prayer.*)

Above all, let us give thanks for Jesus Christ, for his gentleness with little children, for his friendship to young men and maidens, for his love and faith to meet the needs of middle age, and his affection as a refuge for advancing years.

(*Here followeth a period of silent prayer.*)

O thou who art the Word made flesh, full of grace and truth, we claim thee as our Friend and worship thee as our Master. As we come adoring thee in the solitude of our hearts, strengthen us to praise thee openly in generous thought and kindly act; for thy mercy's sake. Amen.

In addition to regular litanies, use can also be made of a litany of prayer and silence, an example of which follows.

A Litany of Prayer and Silence

(*The people seated and bowed, or kneeling.*)

Lord, thou didst make us from the dust of the earth, and didst breathe into our nostrils the breath of life, giving us free and living spirits; teach us how to use our freedom.

(*Here followeth a period of silent prayer.*)

We bless thee that prayer is not mocked, that conscience is not halted by human inability, that our liberty is not mere appearance, but that into our trembling human grasp are placed the issues of life or death in the valley of decision.

(*Here followeth a period of silent prayer.*)

Thou who standest knocking at the door of

every heart, who hast given us the power of judgment and decision, hear us as we pray for emancipation from self.

(*Here followeth a period of silent prayer.*)

Our dispositions are often more than we can master, our tongues speak guile when we would be at peace. Thou who knowest our every infirmity and in whom alone is salvation from weakness and instability, save us in hours when we are rebellious and cannot save ourselves.

(*Here followeth a period of silent prayer.*)

We face our tasks crippled in body, mind, and spirit, we cannot perform our share of labor nor endure our due measure of pain without thy help. We pray not for ease, but for courage; we ask thee not for perfection of body or of mind, but for that strength promised to pure and willing hearts.

(*Here followeth a period of silent prayer.*)

We plead our doubts, but thou art always near, we offer our uncertainty, but always Jesus stands with piercèd hands and feet. How can we deny thee? Give us for our beauty his life's brokenness and pain.

(*Here followeth a period of silent prayer.*)

We offer our heredity as excuse for feeble act and reluctant will, we make excuse that we are not as strong or as resolute as others, we forgive ourselves because of obscure birth or humble position. O thou who hast called thy saints and martyrs from fishers' huts and nameless countrysides, grant us a vision of what life can be, poured out courageously in willing service.

(*Here followeth a period of silent prayer.*)

We have seen ourselves as victims of our day and time, our self-pity has excused us as we have faced new and harder labor and have been confronted with unknown and sinister forces. Thou who didst leave thy followers in the world to face life's darkest nights in the fearlessness of eager faith, grant us thy presence when we would turn back from danger and from toil.

(*Here followeth a period of silent prayer.*)

Our past rises up before us like an armèd man, deeds we deemed buried meet us in the way, thoughts we had put away come back to torment our burdened souls. Thou who didst bring sight to the blind and release to the captive, who didst open the prison house to them that are bound, and didst preach deliverance to the poor and broken-hearted, give us strength to yield our hearts, our minds, our wills to thee; through Jesus Christ, our Lord. Amen.

As the prayer nears its close, the leader turns again to ascription of praise and adoration, using such phrases as "to worthily magnify thy holy name," or "For in thee and in thee only do we put our trust, through Jesus Christ, our Lord."

More beautiful, more significant and more considered prayers will not only better celebrate God and his love, but will dignify and reconstruct the entire service.

The verb should predominate in the prayer, but variety will prevent the petitioners' becoming unduly aware of a certain oft-repeated word, and allow them to pursue the thought uninterruptedly. There are many synonyms which will carry the thought and prevent an interruption, such as give, bestow, grant, trust, confer, bequeath, furnish, supply, help, spare, minister, and a host of other like words, simple, direct, and adequate to convey the meaning. Economy should be exercised in the use of adjectives which clog the flow of thought in prayer as in other public address. Such practice will add clarity and give all the more force to the occasional adjective which is employed.

The use of collects for the opening prayer, if varied and if co-ordinated with the rest of the service, is very helpful. Writing collects is in itself a spiritual discipline of rare value, the economy of words necessitated and the rhythmic and fixed sequence of ideas forming a good habit if one does not find the language and ideas of prayer easily upon his lips. Collects fall in as regular a form as do sonnets. Here is an example:

"O Lord, who hast taught us that all our doings without charity are nothing worth: Send thy Holy Ghost, and pour into our hearts that most excellent gift of charity, the very bond of peace and of all virtues, without which whosoever liveth

is counted dead before thee. Grant this for thine
only Son Jesus Christ's sake. Amen."

The form is always an address to the Deity,
"O God," "O Lord," etc., or some other ascription of praise—"grant," or "do," or "give,"
etc., something, "that" we may do thus and so,
and in the name or for the sake of Jesus
Christ, our Lord, or some similar closing.
Noble public prayer is seldom the product of
spontaneous improvisation, but represents the
highest endeavor of the human spirit, cast in
appropriate literary form.

Although we cannot truly say that we are in
the midst of a recrudescence of mysticism,
nevertheless we can say that there is an increased awareness and desire for the values
which are the fruits of mysticism. One sees
this in the employment of silence in services
in many quarters. There is undoubtedly a
large place in services, where a hurried
sequence carries the worshiper forward, for
moments of utter repose where, with or without direction, men seek in their own way the
contact with God which is the essential element in all worship. We must regain for
Protestantism that quiet and ineffable movement which the devotee feels when alone in
the darkness of a church he kneels before the

figure of the Virgin and listens for the voice of God. There are few services which would not benefit by a moment of silent adoration.

What, then, is the office of music? Music is one of the arts which endeavors along with its sister arts to express that which is too luminous, too high, too holy for the ordinary language of public address. All art came into being as man's effort to express the ineffable qualities he feels in nature, in humanity, and in the realm of the Spirit. When men find ideas which are indescribable in prose, they take brush and chisel in hand to represent and symbolize what they feel, but cannot adequately utter. For the same purpose they employ music, poetry, and architecture. The ordinary language of ordinary day cannot express our most exalted thoughts, and we grasp for a symbol more adequately thus to do.

The hymn is a remarkable combination of poetry and music, and this combination enhances both arts as media of expression. The organ alone can grope for great ideas and clothe them in beauty, but the congregation longs to participate in an act which expresses itself in terms of beauty and aspiration. The hymn, more than the anthem, allows for the element of participation. Good poetry and good music are wed in great hymnology.

The hymn offers more than any other part of the service the emotional outlet which is an essential part of great worship.

What qualities should a hymn have? A hymn should be on a theme worthy of great art and helpful to profound worship.

The hymn should possess feeling, not mere sentiment, but such emotion as surges through "Paradise Lost" or "Paradise Regained." In the presence of that which is celebrated one sees by contrast the depth of his own sin and one's need for purification. The hymn should be objective, not a recital of one's doubts, one's questionings or one's psychological states. It should celebrate affirmatively the qualities of God, Jesus, prayer, faith, repentance, divine grace.

A hymn should be characterized by vitality. It should have a vivid, living, contemporary interest, though couched in the dignified and reverent language of devotion. Even though the language be archaic, if the thought has meaning for the people, it will feed them with the bread of life.

A hymn should be a truthful expression of conviction, not necessarily an analytical theological tractate set to music, but true in the sense that great creeds are true; in fact, a good hymn is a *credo*.

This does not mean that hymns cannot be persuasive; they are persuasive as is great poetry, though speaking in terms of symbolic beauty. Many a doubter is brought back to faith by the quiet on-going persuasiveness of a really great hymn.

An anthem cannot have as intimate a meaning for the worshiper as a hymn, and for that reason should be selected with exceeding care not only from a musical standpoint as a thing in itself, but also for its ethical and spiritual significance and peculiar appropriateness for the particular service in which it is sung. The anthem should be an acclamation of praise, a meditation, an act of contrition, a direction to adoration; it should never be a musical number, never thrown in hit or miss in a service where it is incongruous. It should be picked with great care by both speaker and choirmaster, with the theme of the service in mind. There is a world of difference in an anthem where a score of vocal changes are rung on a single phrase, and a soul-stirring piece such as "Man Shall Give Him Grace and Glory," from Beethoven's "Mount of Olives."

To quicken feelings, to deepen insight, to lift hearts up in adoration, to furnish words of prayer to those otherwise inarticulate, to express humility, to inculcate willingness, to provide a means of expression for those who cannot express themselves—this is the task in which poet and musician combine, for one without the other shall not be made perfect.